THE 'CHRISTIAN' FRINGE

THE 'CHRISTIAN' FRINGE

A critical assessment of
**SEVEN RELIGIOUS ALTERNATIVES
TO MAINSTREAM CHRISTIANITY**
with a Christian response

by
Maurice Burrell

The Canterbury Press
Norwich

© Maurice Burrell 1996

First published 1996 by The Canterbury Press Norwich
(a publishing imprint of Hymns Ancient & Modern Limited,
a registered charity)
St Mary's Works, St Mary's Plain,
Norwich, Norfolk, NR3 3BH

British Library Cataloguing in Publication Data

A catalogue record for this book is available
from the British Library

ISBN 1–85311–116–3

*Typeset by David Gregson Associates
Beccles, Suffolk
and printed and bound in Great Britain by
Biddles Ltd
Guildford and King's Lynn*

Contents

Introduction: Christianity and its Fringe   *page* 1

1. Mormons – The Church of Jesus   13
   Christ of Latter-day Saints

2. Jehovah's Witnesses   43

3. Christadelphians   71

4. The Family – The Children of God   87

5. The Unification Church   97

6. Christian Scientists   109

7. New Age   135

   A Christian Response   157

   Bibliography   171

Introduction:
CHRISTIANITY AND ITS FRINGE

Alongside Christianity and other world religions, at least another five hundred religious movements are active in the United Kingdom today. Their respective memberships range from a handful of people in the smallest groups to hundreds of thousands in the largest. For example, at one end of the spectrum is found the west country based Chrisemma Foundation, with perhaps a dozen followers, meeting in someone's sitting room to receive spiritual counselling from two Enlightened Masters, whilst at the other end of the spectrum are internationally organised groups claiming many thousand of members, meeting in purpose built halls or chapels.

Focusing on only seven of these five-hundred, this book can obviously make no claim to be comprehensive. It is not an encyclopaedia attempting the impossible task of including every religious alternative to mainstream Christianity found in the United Kingdom today. Instead, it treats these seven as representative indicators of the many movements on the fringe of United Kingdom Christianity today.

Why these seven? Any kind of selection is bound to be subjective and, some would say, arbitrary, so the reasons for my choice need to be stated.

(a) Together these seven attract more followers than all other movements on the Christian fringe in the United Kingdom today.

(b) At some time in their lives most people living in the United Kingdom will come into direct (and sometimes face-to-face) contact with one or more of these seven, for these are not a collection of obscure, bizarre and violent sects likely to be known to readers only through the media. On the contrary, they are part and parcel of contemporary religious life.

(c) I have included Jehovah's Witnesses and Mormons for the very obvious reason that almost everyone will have experienced a direct encounter with representatives of these two, probably on their own doorstep.

(d) Christadelphians have found a place because this movement is unique among the established sects in that it was founded by an

1

Englishman, and also because it shares some beliefs with Jehovah's Witneseses and is often confused with them.

(e) Although among the smallest of the groups found in the United Kingdom, the Family (formerly known as the Children of God) and the Unification Church (whose members are often dubbed Moonies) have been included because both have received wide media coverage over the years over claims that they engaged in 'love bombing' proslelytising techniques, which in the case of the Family, it has been alleged, involved the offering of sexual favours to potential converts. Moreover, these two cults have attracted much antagonism from parents who believe their children were 'brainwashed' and needed to be 'rescued' before being 'deprogrammed'.

(f) Christian Science deserves a place because of its beliefs about the unreality of matter, sin, and sickness, and its particular emphasis on spiritual healing.

(g) Quite apart from their individual characteristics, at least six of the seven have sufficient in common to warrant their use as in some sense typical of many of the other groups around the Christian perimeter.

(h) Though very different from the other six, in that it has no unified belief system, no agreed behaviour code, and no single controlling organisation, New Age deserves a place because it probably attracts much more support than all the other groups combined. Moreover, although on the fringe of mainstream Christianity, some of its ideas resonate with some of the thinking found within mainstream churches today.

Four of the seven, Mormons, Jehovah's Witnesses, Christadelphians, and Christian Scientists, have been active in the United Kingdom since the 19th century. The other three, the Family, the Unification Church, and the New Age movement, are much more recent developments in western religious life, though, as we shall see, many of the emphases of New Age religion have been around for some time.

Why the 'Christian' fringe?

Some readers may wish to question my description of these seven as the *Christian* fringe, though they will have noticed that in this book's title 'Christian' is in inverted commas. My justification is that it is around mainstream Christianity rather than one of the other major world religions that these movements hover. They are, therefore, *Christian* in their orientation rather than, say, Hindu, Muslim or Buddhist. Likewise Hinduism, Islam and Buddhism also have their sects and cults, but they are not the subject of this book.

That I place these seven on the Christian fringe should not be taken as a tacit admission on my part that they belong *within* mainstream Christianity itself, or that they share with it a common belief system and code of behaviour. Nothing could be further from the truth. For this much can be said without fear of contradiction. Members of these seven religious movements agree with me that they are not part of mainstream Christianity. In fact, six of the seven believe that their own particular group alone is the true religion and that mainstream Christianity is a distortion of the truth, whilst the seventh thinks it has superseded Christianity. But then the differences begin to appear. I do not agree with either their estimate of mainstream Christianity or of themselves. Six of them do not agree with each other as to which of them is the true manifestation of Christianity, each of them claiming that distinction for itself; and the seventh has little time for either Christianity or for any of the other six.

Mainstream Christianity

Before proceeding further, it may help readers if I clarify the sense in which I am using the term *mainstream*. By mainstream Christianity I mean the kind of Christianity found within the three major divisions of the Christian tradition, Roman Catholicism, Protestantism and Orthodoxy. Although there are many real, obvious and acknowledged differences between these three large Christian traditions, and indeed within them, all three are largely in agreement about the fundamentals of Christian belief.

This general agreement stems from the fact that Roman Catholic, Protestant and Orthodox Christians all accept the Bible as normative in the formation of doctrine. Although they may disagree about precise Bible interpretation, they are united in the view that beliefs may be regarded as *Christian* only insofar as they can be shown to be in agreement with what the Bible teaches. So, for example, H.E.W. Turner wrote in the Church of England Doctrine Commission's Report, *Christian Believing*: 'The Bible remains the basic norm for Christian theology, for it contains not only the record of human search and discovery but also a divine self-disclosure'[1]. Similarly, the *Final Report* of the Anglican Roman Catholic International Commission described the New

Testament as the 'normative record of the authentic foundation of the faith' to which the Christian church must refer its teaching and practice, and added that any attempts to restate Christian doctrine have to be consonant with the apostolic witness recorded in the scriptures.

Mainstream Christians are also in general agreement with the teaching set out in the historic creeds because they believe those creeds are a vital part of the ancient tradition passed on to them and because those creeds faithfully reflect the teaching of scripture. Therefore, Roman Catholics, Protestants and Orthodox Christians all subscribe to the doctrines in those creeds, regarding them as definitive statements of traditional Christianity. It should not surprise readers to find, therefore, that with regard to doctrine the major points of departure between mainstream Christians and the seven alternatives examined in this book revolve very largely around teaching about the Trinity, the Incarnation, and Grace, Faith and Salvation.

Membership figures

Because this book is focusing on seven religious alternatives active in the United Kingdom, rather than further afield, it will be helpful to look at the kind of support mainstream Churches attract compared to the support given to these seven alternatives. According to the 1993/94 edition of *The United Kingdom Christian Handbook*, published by the Christian Research Association, the three mainstream Churches attracting most support in the United Kingdom are the Roman Catholics and the Anglicans, each with just under two million members, and the Presbyterians with 1.2 million. There are also 1.3 million Free Church Christians, Methodists accounting for 459,000 of them, Baptists 230,000, Pentecostals 170,000, Independent Churches 357,000 and others some 131,000. There are a further 276,000 members of Orthodox Churches. This makes a grand total of around 6.7 million people claiming an allegiance to mainstream Christianity in the United Kingdom. In other words, something like 11.5 per cent of the total U.K. population belong to Churches which express their faith in the terms of Christianity's historic creeds. So these all profess a common belief in the one God who has revealed himself as Father, Son and Holy Spirit, and in Jesus Christ, the Incarnate Son of God, who lived, died and rose to be the Saviour of all. That is the sense in which I am using the term 'mainstream Christianity' throughout this book.

As the book proceeds, I shall demonstrate, largely from their own writings, that each of the seven alternatives examined either reject outright these cardinal beliefs of the mainstream or re-write them in such a way as to empty them of their traditional meaning. Before moving on to attempt that task, however, it will help keep the whole matter in some sort of perspective if we compare with those 6.7 million mainstream Christians the membership, insofar as it is known, of these seven alternatives.

Again using figures from the 1993/94 edition of *The United Kingdom Christian Handbook*, the membership of six of the groups examined in this book are as follows: Mormons 145,000, Jehovah's Witnesses 126,000 (though probably as many as 222,000 take part in their activities without being baptised members), Christadelphians 20,000, the Family (the Children of God) 200, the Unification Church 350, and Christian Science 50,000. These figures show that whereas there are some 6.7 million members of mainstream (that is, trinitarian) Churches, the combined total of what are described as non-trinitarian and new religious movements is 437,550 members.

There are no figures for New Age, because there is no central organisation to which members belong, but an intelligent guess would probably quote a figure of several hundred thousand. There are probably many more New Age followers than there are followers of all the other sects, cults and new religious movements put together.

Terminology

Before looking at each of these alternatives in turn, it is necessary to clarify the terminology used to describe them. Forty years ago, *Christian Deviations*, a book written by Horton Davies, a church history lecturer at Mansfield and Regent's Park Colleges, Oxford, was required reading for theological students. Published by SCM, and sub-titled 'Essays in Defence of the Christian Faith', it was a serious attempt to examine what the author called 'distortions' or 'rivals' of Christianity. The author's aim was to demonstrate as clearly as possible the main points of departure between historic Christianity and Christian deviations, 'deviations' being Davies' description of the kind of movements which I am designating as belonging to *The 'Christian' Fringe*. Davies pointed out that it was from mainstream Christian beliefs and practices that these other movements were deviating, and because of that they deserved the title 'Christian Deviations'. For some years after publication, 'Christian deviations' became the acceptable designation among Christians for such alternatives to mainstream Christianity.

Thirty five years before the publication of *Christian Deviations*, Ernst Troeltsch had argued that the Christian doctrine of the Trinity had resulted in three main types of sociological development of Christian thought, the Church, the sect, and mysticism.[2] Modifying Troeltsch's ideas, Richard Niebuhr argued for Church, sect and denomination as a more accurate analysis of this sociological development, claiming that sects which survived the death of their charismatic founders were transformed into denominations.[3] Bryan Wilson disagreed with Niebuhr's assertion that persisting sects always became denominations, arguing that sects which persisted were better described as established sects.

Until fairly recently, most sociological writers have followed the trend describing alternatives to mainstream religion as 'sects' and many have gone along with Wilson in writing of sects which persisted after the death of their charismatic leaders as 'established sects'. Sociologists felt that 'sect' was a more neutral term than some of the other terms, in itself passing no judgement on the movement being studied. Some mainstream Christian writers, being unconcerned about sociological detachment, often referred to such groups as 'cults' and sometimes as 'modern heresies', descriptions which carried with them definite judgmental overtones, though many still preferred Davies' 'Christian deviations'. Now, promoted by contemporary sociologists like Eileen Barker, the term 'New Religious Movements' (often abbreviated to NRMs) is in vogue. Even that is not without its critics, who argue that it implies that all the groups thus categorised are 'new' and 'religions', neither of which is always true.

I shall make use of most of these terms, as well as 'Christian fringe' and 'alternatives to mainstream Christianity'. Moreover, as a practising Christian within the mainstream (and as an ordained Anglican who is therefore in some sense an official representative of at least that part of the mainstream), I shall not pretend to be neutral. The fact is that we all bring our own subjective views into whatever topic we discuss, no matter how objective we like to think we are, whether we are sociologists, theologians, or anything else, and I am no different. Nevertheless, I shall do my best to be honest and accurate in my portrayal of those whose beliefs and practices I do not share.

'Sect' is my preferred description of the larger established alternatives to the mainstream, founded in the United States in the 19th century and planted in Great Britain soon afterwards. Four examples of such established sects, Jehovah's Witnesses, Mormons, Christadelphians, and Christian Scientists, are examined in this book.

I prefer 'cult', on the other hand, when referring to those fairly young movements whose members unquestioningly follow a strong charismatic leader. The leader usually makes great demands of them and requires their full obedience and loyalty. The Family and the Unification Church (often called the Moonies), are my two examples of cults included in this book.

The seventh group, New Age, defies definition as either a sect or a cult. Indeed, it can be argued that it is has become a loose federation of a number of sects and cults, all of which shelter under its great umbrella, and each of which could be examined separately.

Authority

No matter how we describe such groups, their most obvious characteristic is their rejection of mainstream Christianity. This is followed inevitably by their deviation from some of Christianity's beliefs and practices. In that sense, therefore, Horton Davies description of them as *Christian Deviations* has not yet outlived its usefulness.

Sociologists have long recognised this rejection as a common characteristic of all such religious alternatives. According to Betty Scarf, a sect is a group holding religious beliefs which 'diverge in some aspects radically from those of existing religious groups or of the secular world'. The divergence may be in the realm of doctrine or ethics, or it may concern scientific or political matters.[4] Bryan Wilson focuses more specifically on the issue of authority. For him sects are movements of religious protest: the form of the protest may vary from sect to sect but is always marked by the rejection of the authority of mainstream religious leaders and sometimes of the secular government as well.[5]

That this question of authority is a key issue in the mainstream/alternatives discussion becomes clear as we consider our seven movements. Five of them, Jehovah's Witnesses, Christadelphians, Christian Scientists, the Family and the Unification Church, reject mainstream Christianity on the grounds that the mainstream has rejected the Bible's teachings and has replaced them with man-made tradition. In dealing with the Bible itself, however, these five alternatives face exactly the same problem as mainstream Christians about how the Bible is to be interpreted, and each has its own way of handling it.

Jehovah's Witnesses and Christian Scientists reject the idea of private interpretation and do not encourage unguided Bible study. For them authority for interpreting the Bible lies solely with their own God guided leaders, who tell them what the Bible means. Similarly, the Unification Church believes it is impossible to interpret the Bible correctly without divine help, for it is written in difficult code language which needs to be deciphered. Members are pointed to a particular book, *Divine Principle*, for the correct answers. The Family, though taking a fundamentalist attitude to the Bible, believe the writings of their founder, David Berg, are essential for a proper understanding of the Bible, so Berg's *Mo-letters* become the standard of truth for all members. The Christadelphians look to the doctrinal tradition handed down from former leaders and current Christadelphian publications as indications of true Bible interpretation.

All five are examples of what the Lutheran writer, Kurt Hutten, as described sects with a Bible in the left hand. Referring to the ordination of a Swedenborgian minister, who was required to hold a Bible in the right hand and one of Swedenborg's books in his left hand, Hutten claimed that every sect had a Bible in the left hand, that is, another source of authority used to interpret (and often to supersede) the teaching of the Bible itself.[6]

Mormons go a stage further than these five, asserting that the Bible is inadequate as a source of truth because it is incomplete. Mainstream Churches cannot teach God's full truth, therefore, because they possess only part of it – an incomplete Bible. Mormons claim that, in contrast, the full divine revelation has been given to the world through their founder and prophet, Joseph Smith, and that three of his books provide the additional scriptures which the world needs to discover the full Christian Gospel.

New Age rejects mainstream authority in other ways, being syncretistic and happily holding together teaching from many traditions alongside Christianity. New Age writers believe that Christianity belongs to the Age of Pisces which is being superseded by the Age of Aquarius. The New Age implication is clear. The old must give way to the new. Christianity has outlived its usefulness.

Leadership

Closely allied with the rejection of the authority of mainstream Christianity is the special place afforded to leaders by alternative religions. Max Weber, the eminent sociologist, drew attention to this trait, pointing out that the founder of a sect displayed what could best be described as charismatic authority over his followers. The leader was believed to be set apart from ordinary mortals and to be endowed with supernatural, superhuman, or at least very exceptional powers or qualities. Because of his 'divinely inspired mission, his heroic deeds, his extraordinary endowments',[7] he was able to demand and get obedience from his disciples. Weber went on to show that, following the charismatic leader's death, if the sect continued, then a process of routinisation followed, resulting in the development of a bureaucratic structure with power being shared between those who headed the organisation. Five of the seven movements in this book exemplify one or more stages in that process. One has a living charismatic leader, three have moved from charismatic to bureaucratic leadership, and one is in the process of making that transition. The two others do not fit easily into Weber's classification.

The Unification Church has as its living charismatic leader Sun Myung Moon, whom it believes to be a Messianic figure, the Lord of the Second Advent, whose God-given task is to what the Lord of the First Advent, Jesus Christ, failed to achieve two-thousand years ago. Because of this, members are often referred to as 'Moonies'.

Mormons (strictly speaking the Church of Jesus Christ of Latter-day Saints), Jehovah's Witnesses, and Christian Scientists are three established sects which have made the transition from charismatic leaders to bureaucratic leadership. Mormons still regard their long deceased founder, Joseph Smith, as God's mouthpiece. Soon after his murder in 1844, his followers, led by another charismatic figure Brigham Young, began the long trek across America where they were to found the Mormon state of Utah and begin to build up the strong bureaucratic structure through which the contemporary Mormon Church works. Although their president still has a powerful position as Smith's successor and God's prophet and spokesman, he exercises his authority within a strong organisation. Following the death of their founder, Charles Taze Russell, Jehovah's Witnesses began to stress the importance of the Watch Tower Society. The Society's seven Directors, who are now believed to speak on Jehovah's behalf, control the movement from its Brooklyn headquarters in the United States. Similarly, Christian Scientists are governed by a Board of Directors in Boston. Nevertheless, through them the Christian Science founder, Mary Baker Eddy, continues to exercise a kind of posthumous authority.

The single example in this book of a movement in the process of making the transition from charismatic leader through routinisation to bureaucracy is the Family (The Children of God). Until their founder David Berg's death in 1994, the Family believed that in Berg they had a charismatic leader who communed directly with God and was able to command total obedience. It is too early yet to predict whether they will develop a bureaucratic leadership pattern similar to those of Mormons, Jehovah's Witnesses, and Christian Scientists or whether they will fail to survive.

The leadership style of the small Christadelphian movement and the large New Age movement remain to be considered.

Unlike most of the other sects, Christadelphians never regarded their founder, John Thomas as anything other than a good Bible-believing leader who with God's help was able to show them the errors of the mainstream Christianity from which they had parted. His influence was crucial and formative, but Christadelphians have never believed it to be infallible. After his death Roberts, Andrew, and other leaders emerged, but they too were never regarded as anything other than good men whose views should be treated seriously. No strong controlling central organisation ever emerged, although in the United Kingdom the Birmingham congregation exercised considerable influence. Only in the loosest sense is there a central organisation to which Christadelphians belong. The dominating force in this movement is the distinctive attitude to the Bible which all Christadelphians share. There is no allegiance to any particular leader, or to any central hierarchy or organisation.

The case of the New Age movement is more complicated, for 'New Age' has become a kind of umbrella term under which shelters all kinds of ideas and beliefs, some of which stem from earlier movements which have had very strong leadership, and others from a string of influential figures of national and international reputation. Their style of leadership, however, is usually very different from that exercised in movements founded by charismatic leaders, being largely by gentle influence.

The author's stance

Before considering these seven alternatives to mainstream Christianity, a general comment about my own stance may be helpful. My method in dealing with all seven is the same. I show (as far as possible) how each originated, outline what its adherents believe and practise, and describe how each movement seeks to spread its views. I then point out the fundamental differences between each group and mainstream Christianity, so there is a section in every chapter showing where that group and mainstream Christianity part company.

Brought up in an age that seems to believe that the greatest commandment is 'Thou shalt not be intolerant', some readers may not take kindly to my approach. 'What matters most is sincerity', they may wish to argue, 'especially in religion'. I ask them to bear with me, for I do agree with them about the importance of both tolerance and sincerity. Unlike some writers, I have found no reason to question the basic sincerity of members of any of these seven movements. Some of them have gone out of their way to explain their beliefs to me, and have invariably treated me with courtesy. For my part, I have come to respect them, even though I have had a nagging suspicion that they have put up with my questioning only because they have seen me as a potential convert. I remain convinced that those I have met are utterly sincere. Christianity, however, is about truth as well as sincerity, and this is where I have found it necessary to part company with them, and, I may add, they with me.

Whatever the horrific Jonestown, Waco and Solar Temple incidents have to teach us, and the lessons are still being pondered, they at least demonstrate that sincerity and truth do not necessarily go hand in hand. It is all too possible to be completely sincere and yet terribly wrong. Inherent in the belief systems of all who died in the Jonestown People's Temple, with the Davidians at Waco, and with the Order of the Solar Temple in Switzerland was not a lack of sincerity but a lack of truth. It was this fundamental flaw which led to such awful consequences. I am not suggesting that any similarities exist in the activities of the various groups dealt with in this book. What is clear, however, is that without truth sincerity is inadequate and may be positively harmful. This book is one person's attempt to get at the truth. I am in no way claiming to be a perfect judge of truth, but I hope that I have dealt with those with whom I have found it necessary to part company with both accuracy and sensitivity

REFERENCES

1. page 115.
2. E. Troletsch, *Social Teachings of the Christian Churches*, Vol.1, pages 331ff.
3. H. Richard Niebuhr, *The Social Sources of Denominationalism*, page 19.
4. B. Scharf, *The Sociological Study of Religion*, page 113.
5. Bryan Wilson, *Religious Sects*, page 7.
6. Kurt Hutten, *Die Glaubenswelt die Secktierers*, page 104, cited A. Hoekema, *The Four Major Cults*, page 378.
7. Max Weber, *The Theory of Social and Economic Organisation*, page 358.

Chapter 1

MORMONS

The Church of Jesus Christ
of Latter-day Saints

There are some six million Mormons in the world, meeting in more than 15,000 congregations in 122 countries. The Mormon Church (or the Church of Jesus Christ of Latter-day Saints, to give it its correct title) claims that its 32,000 missionaries make about 216,000 converts a year and that its overall membership is growing by 6.6 per cent annually. It has tripled its membership in the last twenty-five years and expects to achieve a target of eleven million members by the year 2000.

The British figures are even more spectacular, with an increase from under 20,000 in 1960 to about 150,000 today. There are now 400 Mormon congregations and 225 chapels in the United Kingdom. A recent Mormon publication claimed that, during the last decade, a new congregation has been created every fortnight, a new chapel has been completed every four weeks, and membership is growing by around 5,000 new members each year.

THE MORMON CLAIM

'The most distinguising feature of the Church of Jesus Christ of Latter-day Saints is divine authority by direct revelation.' So wrote David McKay, perhaps the most effective leader of the Mormons since Joseph Smith and Brigham Young. McKay added, 'There are those who claim authority through historical descent, others from the scriptures, but this Church stands out as making the distinctive claim that the authority of the priesthood has come directly from God the Father and the Son, by revelation to Joseph Smith.'[1]

No one can begin to understand Mormonism without getting to grips with this basic concept. It is set out in two of the Mormon Church's Thirteen Articles of belief. 'We believe the Bible to be the World of God, as far as it is translated correctly. We also believe the Book of Mormon to be the Word of God' (Article 1). 'We believe all that God has revealed, all

13

that He does now reveal, and we believe that He will yet reveal many great and important things pertaining to the Kingdom of God' (Article 9).

Working from that credal starting point, the Morman Church has developed a doctrine of continual and progressive revelation which, in effect, asserts three things:

1. The Bible is the Word of God, so far as it is translated correctly.
2. The inspired utterances of Joseph Smith, as the Mormon Church's first President, Prophet, Seer and Revelator, are the Word of God.
3. The inspired utterances of Smith's successors down through the years are the Word of God, for each Mormon leader, in his turn, is believed to be the Church's President, Prophet, Seer and Revelator.

It is significant that although Mormons claim to accept the Bible as the Word of God in so far as it is translated correctly, they make no such qualification regarding *The Book of Mormon*. They claim that the manner in which *The Book of Mormon* was translated ruled out the possibility of error. This is a strange claim when it is remembered that, quite apart from the way in which the alleged translation took place, some 3,000 changes have been made in the text since the book's first appearance in 1830.[2]

Mormons do acknowledge the Bible as one of their governing scriptures. Because of their doctrine of continual and progressive revelation, however, in practice the Bible takes second place to the additional scriptures which they claim to have received through Joseph Smith, namely *The Book of Mormon*, *Doctrine and Covenants*, and *Pearl of Great Price*.

Distinctive Mormon beliefs are derived from these additional scriptures, not from the Bible. That is why Le Grand Richards, one of the most important recent Mormon writers, claimed that Mormonism did not depend upon the Bible for its teaching. 'If we had no Bible', he added, 'we would still have all the needed direction and information through the revelation of the Lord "to his servants the prophets" in these latter-days.'[3]

Christians need to be very clear about this fundamental difference between the mainstream Christian churches and Mormons. To Mormons their additional scriptures are absolute necessities, whereas the Bible, though important, is an optional extra, containing a partial and inadequate revelation for God's people living today. Mormonism stands or falls on the validity of this claim. To understand how Mormons arrived at this view, we need to delve briefly into the short but tempestuous life of Joseph Smith, the Mormon founder.

JOSEPH SMITH

Visions, Gold Plates, Supernatural Spectacles

Born on 23rd December 1805 at Sharon, Windsor County, in the State of Vermont, USA, Joseph Smith was the fourth child of Joseph and Lucy Smith. Smith's grandfather, Solomon Mack, had written an autobiography telling of his dramatic conversion to the Christian faith and containing some of his own hymns. His uncle, Jason Mack, had founded a religious community governed on communistic lines. Charges and counter-charges have been made by non-Mormons and Mormons about the moral standing of Smith's family. Leaving all these aside, one thing seems certain. The Mormon founder was raised in a family with a strong belief in the supernatural but which sat lightly to traditional Christianity.

The future Mormon prophet spent most of his childhood in New York State, first at Palmyra in County Ontario, and then at the nearby Manchester. A religious revival led by a Methodist named Lane was then affecting the whole of the State. The latest of a number of 'awakenings' that had become quite common in 19th century America, Lane's revival achieved dramatic results and most Christian churches began to welcome a steady influx of converts. Some of Smith's relatives became Presbyterians and he himself was attracted to Methodism. He remained uncertain which church to join, however, for like most other people he was confused by the multiplicity of denominations all claiming people's allegiance.

During this time of personal uncertainty, Joseph Smith claimed to receive the first of a series of visions. In 1820, and as a direct answer to his prayer for God's guidance, God the Father and his Son Jesus Christ appeared to the fifteen years old Smith in a pillar of light. God told him to join none of the existing Christian denominations because their creeds were an abomination in God's sight and they had all become apostate. Instead, Joseph was told that he was to be used by God to restore real Christianity and the true Church to the earth.

Three years later Smith received a second vision. An angelic being named Moroni told him of the whereabouts of certain gold plates containing the history of the former inhabitants of the American continent and the fullness of the Christian Gospel. The plates were said to be buried in a stone box on the side of a hill called Cumorah, near Palmyra. Though the writing on the plates was in the form of ancient hieroglyphics, the uneducated young Smith would be able to translate them with the help of two supernaturally provided transparent stones set in silver bows. When he read the plates through these supernatural 'spectacles', he would be able to understand the meaning of the hieroglyphics. Smith claimed that the vision was repeated several times and that on each occasion he was able to see exactly where the plates were buried. At the same time he was promised, 'Behold, I will reveal unto you the Priesthood, by the hand of Elijah the Prophet, before the coming of the great and terrible day of the Lord'.[4]

Smith said that on 22nd September 1823 he went to the designated spot and found the box containing the plates. The eight inch square plates were bound together by three large rings. The supernatural 'spectacles' were by their side. When the eager Smith reached into the cavity to remove the plates, however, a supernatural power immobilised his arm. Following three unsuccessful attempts to remove the plates, he cried out in frustration, 'Why cannot I obtain this book?' Reappearing, the angelic visitor told him that his failure was because of his disobedience and his wish to make money out of his discovery. If Smith repented and remained faithful to God, he would be allowed to remove the plates at a later date. For the next four years, on the exact anniversary of Moroni's first visit, Smith returned to the hill Cumorah, met Moroni, and received further instructions about the plates. Then on 22nd September 1827, when he was twenty-one years old, he was allowed to unearth the plates and the 'spectacles' and take them away.

The Book of Mormon

Joseph Smith says he began translating the plates almost at once. Martin Harris, a friendly farmer who had given him money, acted as his scribe, writing down what Smith dictated as he looked at the plates through the 'spectacles'. Harris took a copy of some of the characters and Smith's translation of them to Professor Charles Anthon of Columbia University. Smith claimed that Anthon confirmed both their authenticity and the accuracy of his translation and Mormons still cite Anthon's testimony as evidence of *The Book of Mormon*'s authenticity. Smith completed his translation in 1829 and published *The Book of Mormon* on 18th March 1830. He claimed that the plates were then handed back to Moroni. They have not been seen since.

The Book of Mormon is named after a General Mormon who is said to have lived on the American continent about AD 400. There he kept the records of his ancestors and then entrusted them to his son, Moroni, for safe keeping. Moroni buried the plates in the ground. Mormons believe these were the plates unearthed by Smith in 1827 and that Moroni, by this time a resurrected being, was the divine messenger who told Smith where they were hidden.

The book has two major themes. First, it tells the story of the descendants of a prophet named Lehi, who left Jerusalem with his family some 600 years before Christ and reached America. There he became the founding father of a mighty civilisation. The Indians whom Columbus found when he discovered America centuries later are said to be 'the benighted remnant' of this once mighty civilisation. Mormons claim that the book has a historical span covering the years from 600 BC to AD 400. Secondly, *The Book of Mormon* also contains a fuller Gospel than that found in the Bible. It gives an account of a visit Christ is said to have made to America following his death and resurrection in Palestine and shows Christ repeating much of the teaching previously given to the original apostles and other disciples, including the Sermon on the Mount.

Apart from Joseph Smith himself, eleven people are claimed as witnesses to the existence of the gold plates and their translation. Their sworn statements appear at the front of every copy of the book.

The Restored Church and its Priesthood

During the 1823 visions, Moroni is said to have informed Smith that the true Priesthood, forfeited centuries earlier by an apostate Church, was about to be restored through Smith. It is claimed that the promise was fulfilled soon afterwards. According to Smith, John the Baptist came from heaven to confer the Aaronic Priesthood on him and Oliver Cowdery, and they then baptised and ordained each other. Later, Peter, James, and John likewise came from heaven to confer on them the superior Melchizedek Priesthood and to appoint them first and second elders in the Church.

On 6th April 1830, Smith and five supporters founded the Church of Jesus Christ of Latter-day Saints in a house at Fayette. A further revelation instructed Church members to receive Smith's teaching as authoritative, God saying of the prophet, 'His word ye shall receive, as if from mine own mouth'.[5]

Growth and Opposition

One of Smith's early acts was to appoint twelve apostles and make them responsible for missionary outreach. This quickly brought results, membership soon increasing from a mere handful to several hundreds.

Not everyone believed Smith, however, and he and his followers faced ridicule and opposition, often from members of the mainstream Christian churches. Some of the first Mormon missionaries found that the people of Ohio were more receptive to the Mormon message and soon Mormons began to settle in that state, where Kirtland became their stronghold from 1831 to 1838.

More Scriptures

Smith claimed to receive many more direct revelations from God, most of them concerning the new Church's organisation and leadership. Counsellors, apostles, high priests, bishops, elders, and missionaries, were all appointed in this way and despatched to their various duties. A divine revelation was received giving instructions for the building of the first Mormon Temple in Kirtland. Another designated Ohio as the new Zion where the faithful were to gather. It seems that whenever Smith wished his followers to accept some new doctrine or regulations concerning the organisation of the growing Mormon movement, he received a timely revelation which gave his words divine authority. Plans were soon in hand to preserve all these revelations in print. *Doctrine and Covenants* contains all 133 of the revelations Smith claimed to receive between September 1823 and July 1843. They include the well-known abstinence rule 6, instructing Mormons to abstain from tobacco, alcohol, and tea and coffee, and to eat meat only in moderation.

The most far-reaching and controversial revelation was section 132. In it the Mormon leader tried to justify his unorthodox views concerning marriage. He made two claims.

First, Smith said that ordinary marriage came to an end when one of the partners died. If the partners made a marriage covenant for eternity, however, they would be reunited after the resurrection. Because of this belief, Mormons have a temple ceremony known as celestial marriage to ensure that their marriages will survive physical death. The ceremony also qualifies participants for the highest grade of salvation.

Smith's second claim was more controversial. He said that God had given him the right to practise polygamy and to tell his followers to do the same. There is evidence that Smith and some of his followers had begun to practise polygamy long before this 'revelation' and that the revelation was proclaimed to justify their actions.

As we shall see, government pressure forced the Mormons to give up polygamy in 1890. The polygamy question is still important, however, because of its bearing upon the Mormon view of scripture. Because section 132 is still printed in *Doctrine and Covenants*, Mormons regard it as scripture. Paradoxically, however, it is a part of scripture which must not be obeyed on pain of excommunication. Some Mormons argue that polygamy was an interim arrangement, designed for a time when they were a very small minority and when they needed plural marriages to bring about a rapid increase in the number of Mormon children. Others claim that as law-abiding citizens they had no option but to obey the law of the land. Whatever rationalisation occurs, however, the inconsistency of the Mormon position remains. If Smith was right in proclaiming section 132 as a God-given revelation, then polygamy should have continued no matter what the cost. Clearly, if the choice is between obeying God and obeying the secular authority, obedience to God ought to come first. Of course if Smith was wrong, no problem exists for non-Mormons. For obvious reasons, Mormons cannot admit that their founder was in error, for if he could be mistaken in this revelation, who could say he was right in the others? And if he were proved unreliable in *Doctrine and Covenants*, to what extent could the other Mormon scriptures be trusted?

Pearl of Great Price completes the Mormon scriptures. It contains the Authorised Version of Matthew 24 with a few minor variations and Smith's version of some of the early chapters of Genesis. There is also an alleged translation from a papyrus said to have been discovered in the Egyptian catacombs. Smith claimed it contained the writings of Abraham when in Egypt.

The Kirtland Bank Collapse

Smith's idea of an earthly Zion based in Ohio was not to be realised, for anti-Mormon feeling began to develop in that State. Even the prophet was not immune to ill-treatment and at Hiram he was beaten and tarred and feathered by an angry mob. Mormons have always maintained, with some justification, that the opposition was stirred up by the mainstream Christian denominations to force Mormons to move elsewhere. There were, however, some more mundane causes. Mormons began to outnumber non-Mormons in some places. People envied Mormon success in controlling local industry and commerce. The Mormon habit of dubbing all non-Mormons as 'Gentiles' made them even less popular. Resentment further increased as non-Mormon families began to be disrupted by conversions to the Mormon faith.

The major cause of anti-Mormonism, however, was the failure of a bank Smith had started to raise money for the Temple and for various industrial and commercial enterprises. Many people lost large sums when they tried to redeem the bank notes Smith had issued. Smith was fined $1,000 for operating the bank illegally. A number of law suits followed. Some have estimated that Smith ran up debts of some $150,000. This disastrous episode brought about a crisis of authority within the Mormon Church. Five of the original Twelve Apostles broke with Smith. Three of them formed another church, declared that Smith was a fallen prophet, and branded him and his loyal followers as heretics.

Polygamy and Murder

The Mormons moved to Missouri, where Independence became their new headquarters and where they began to build another temple. It was not long, however, before the local people began to object to Mormon anti-slavery views. As Mormon numbers increased there was also a growing concern about their political power. In the disturbances that ensued, two non-Mormons were killed and the state governor ordered out the Missouri militia. Eventually Smith and some of his supporters were arrested and sentenced to death. The general ordered to carry out the sentence refused, believing the Mormons to be innocent, so the prisoners were released.

The Mormons moved on to Illinois where they founded the city of Nauvoo and built yet another temple. Smith and some of his followers had begun to practise polygamy in the 1830s and it became more common among Mormons in Nauvoo. At first, Smith tried to keep the practice secret, but when it became public knowledge some of his disillusioned associates wrote against what they regarded as his immorality in a newspaper called the Nauvoo Expositor. Acting as mayor of Nauvoo, Smith ordered their printing office to be destroyed. They promptly appealed to the state governor and Smith, his brother, and two other Mormon leaders were arrested and remanded in custody to await trial. The trial never took place. An excited mob stormed the prison, the guards made only a half-hearted attempt to repel them, and Smith was shot dead.

Some would say that the enraged mob that lynched Smith did more to further the Mormon cause than any number of Mormon missionaries. 'The martyrdom gave to the story of Joseph Smith the imperishable force of tragedy. What was already a legend it converted into an epic ... And it was the legend of Joseph Smith, from which all evidences of deception, ambition and marital excesses were gradually obliterated, that became the great cohesive force within the Church.'[6]

AN EXAMINATION OF THE MORMON CLAIMS

Mormons and non-Mormons can agree on at least this: Mormonism stands or falls on the genuineness of the Mormon claims about Joseph Smith. Was Smith telling the truth about his visions, the plates, and their translation? Was he a fraud who invented the story for personal gain? Was he, perhaps, a sadly deluded man who was sincere but wrong? We must consider the evidence.

Where is the Manuscript Evidence?

An obvious question to ask is, Where are the plates today? The Mormon reply that they were returned to Moroni and have not been seen since, seems too easy a way out of a very difficult situation.

Mormons sometimes argue that Christians do not possess the original manuscripts of the Bible. While this is true, there are many ancient biblical manuscripts that are available to the eye of honest, scholarly examination. Despite the fact that Smith claimed to have copied characters from the plates and sent them to Professor Anthon, there appear to be no Mormon copies available for critical assessment. The absence of such evidence is a very strong argument against the Mormon claim.

What did Anthon really say?

Smith claimed that Professor Anthon vouched for the authenticity of the characters Smith copied from the gold plates. Anthon's version is very different. In a letter written to E.D. Howe in 1834, the professor stated, 'The whole story about my having pronounced the Mormonite inscription to be "reformed Egyptian hieroglyphics" is perfectly false'. Anthon agreed that a man did bring him a piece of paper containing what he described as a 'singular scrawl' and which he believed had been copied from a book containing various alphabets. At first, Anthon thought it was a hoax and treated the story rather light-heartedly. When the man told him about the gold plates and mentioned that he had been asked for money to help publish the translation, Anthon concluded that it was 'a scheme to cheat the farmer of his money'.[7]

Mormons claim that originally Anthon had backed the Mormon story but later anti-Mormon prejudice made him change his mind. It is hard to find a motive for such action. Would a well-known professor risk his reputation because of blind prejudice against the Mormons? Even if this were conceivable, the Mormons are still faced with a paradoxical situation. On the one hand, they claim Anthon was trustworthy when witnessing to the authenticity of the copied characters. On the other hand, they say he was lying when he wrote his letter to Howe. If the Mormon version of the incident is true, it raises questions about Anthon's reliability to vouch for the inscription in the first place. If Anthon's version is true, the Mormons have no independent evidence to substantiate their claim about the characters.

What kind of a person was Smith?

The aim of this book is not to attack the Mormon founder's morality. People living in ecclesiastical glass houses should not throw stones. Seen historically and in his particular North American environment, he was certainly no worse, and probably a lot better, than many members of Christian denominations who persecuted him and his followers. Nevertheless, when a person makes special claims and asserts that they have a divine origin, it is right to consider the kind of person he was.

Mormons have always claimed that Joseph Smith was simply telling the story as it happened. Others have provided different explanations. From the start, some maintained that Smith and his chief associates were conspirators who invented the stories and foisted them upon a gullible public. Smith's own father-in-law, Isaac Hale, described him as, a liar and a cheat. Others have argued that Smith had a vivid imagination and ended up believing his own story. Fawn Brodie described him as 'nimble-witted, ambitious, and gifted with a boundless imagination'. She said he had an extraordinary capacity for fantasy and an 'undisciplined imagination'. She added that for Smith the 'line between truth and fiction was always blurred'.[8] It also has to be remembered that Smith was about fifteen when he received the first vision and seventeen at the time of the second. Age alone does not rule out the possibility that the visions were genuine, but it has to be kept in mind when assessing their value.

Can we trust the eleven witnesses?

Every copy of *The Book of Mormon* contains sworn statements from eleven witnesses to its authenticity. The first three, Oliver Cowdery, David Whitmer and Martin Harris, said, 'We ... have seen the plates ... we also know that they have been translated by the gift and power of God, for his voice hath declared it unto us.' Another eight claimed that Smith showed them the gold plates and allowed them to handle them.

Regarding the first three, it has to be remembered that they were among Smith's first supporters and, like him, were anxious that the new movement should succeed. Their testimony is somewhat undermined by the fact that all three later left the Mormon Church and were then branded as thieves and counterfeiters by other Mormons. Moreover, in 1837 Whitmer led a faction in an attempt to overthrow Smith's leadership. Would they have acted in this way if they really believed what they said about the plates?

Concerning the testimony of the eight, it is worth remembering that three of them were Whitmers and three were Smiths. Non-Mormons have always regarded this as too close a family circle.

What about the archaeological evidence?

The Book of Mormon maintains that:

- Two great civilisations once existed on the American continent;
- Millions of people populated that part of the earth;
- All of this began with the exodus of a small group of people from Israel many years before Christ.

What do archaeologists make of such claims? 'Leading archaeological researchers have not only repudiated the claims of *The Book of Mormon* as to the existence of these civilisations, but have adduced considerable evidence to show the impossibility of the accounts given in the Mormon Bible.'[9] 'I do not believe that there is a single thing of value concerning the pre-history of the American Indian in *The Book of Mormon* and I believe the great majority of American archaeologists would agree with me.'[10]

Why does *The Book of Mormon* contain so much of the Authorised Version of the Bible?

The book is supposed to cover the period from 600 BC to AD 400. Whoever compiled it, however, appears to have had a copy of the 1611 Authorised Version before him. Comparisons of Isaiah 2-14 and 2 Nephi 12-24, Isaiah 48-49 and 2 Nephi 20-21, and Malachi 3-4 and 3 Nephi 24-25 are most revealing in this respect. Many more instances of this 'borrowing' occur throughout *The Book of Mormon*. How do Mormons explain this? They argue that, because Smith knew the language of the Authorised Version so well, it was inevitable that he would use such language in his translation. This really will not do. *The Book of Mormon* does not just contain occasional AV-sounding phrases and verses but rather whole blocks, sometimes many chapters, of actual AV material. The book also has some of the established inaccuracies of the Authorised Version. No matter how Mormons try to avoid the obvious conclusion, the facts speak for themselves. Whoever wrote *The Book of Mormon* had the Authorised Version of the Bible (or a book containing many quotations from it) before him. This completely demolishes the Mormon claim that the book in its original form was completed around AD 400.

Are the claims of *The Book of Mormon* reasonable?

The Book of Mormon claims that a detailed Christian theology was being proclaimed as early as the sixth century before Christ? Mormons expect us to believe that, whereas the Old Testament writers foresaw the coming of Christ in dark shadows, *The Book of Mormon* was able to record detailed visions in which most of the events of Christ's early life shone as brightly as the noonday sun.[11]

These include:
• the virgin birth;
• the divine sonship of Christ;
• the baptism of Jesus by John the Baptist;
• Christ's ministry of teaching and healing;
• His fellowship with the twelve apostles;
• His atoning death on the cross;
• His triumphant resurrection.

Good though it is to read about such things in *The Book of Mormon*, it does not seem likely that they could have been written down 600 years before they actually happened – and, what is more, in the language of AD 1611. Mormons say the writer is setting out this theology prophetically to prepare for Christ's first coming. A more reasonable explanation is that *The Book of Mormon* is a product of the nineteenth century AD.

The Mormon myth

Some well-meaning Christians have tried to help Mormons by suggesting that we do Mormonism a disservice by taking the Mormon claims literally and then raising intellectual arguments against them. Instead, we should treat the story of angelic visitations, gold plates and supernatural spectacles, as part of the great Mormon myth. What matters is not whether the story is literally true, but rather whether it is a good literary vehicle for an essentially religious message.

Far from finding this attitude helpful, the Mormon leadership will have no truck with it. To them the whole story is literally true and has to be swallowed hook, line and sinker. It is true that some younger contemporary Mormons are finding it difficult to continue to take the prophet's claims at their face value. Thomas O'Dea argued that although the Mormon fundamentalists seem to control the Church today, there are great tensions between these leaders and some of the younger Mormon intellectuals. He thought these intellectuals would either change the Church or leave it.[14] However that may work out in the future, the present position is quite clear. The Mormon religion stands or falls on the Mormon claims about the origin, discovery and translation of *The Book of Mormon.*

The evidence presented in the previous pages demonstrates the hollowness of those claims. Whatever else *The Book of Mormon* may or may not be, it is certainly not what Mormons from 1830 to the present day have alleged it to be. Heavenly visions, gold plates, magical spectacles, mysterious writing, and disappearing evidence make a good story – but it reads more like fiction than like fact.

BRIGHAM YOUNG

Brigham Young succeeded Smith as Mormon leader in 1847. Born in June 1801 at Whitingham in Vermont, he had been brought up as a Methodist, but after reading *The Book of Mormon* he became a Mormon in 1832. He soon became active in missionary work, numbering his own family among his first converts.

Mission to Britain

Seven years before he became Mormon leader, Great Britain felt the impact of Smith's dynamic successor. Docking at Liverpool in April 1840, he completely transformed the Church within a year. The first Mormon missionaries had arrived in 1837. They won a handful of converts and founded the first Mormon Church outside the United States at Preston. This then became the centre of a missionary drive to the rest of the country, but progress was slow. The situation changed dramatically with Young's arrival. He dispatched missionaries to strategic points in Britain. By the middle of 1841 there were 5,000 Mormons in the British Isles. Ten years later the numbers had increased to 30,000.

One of the most significant results of Young's visit was his organisation of the emigration of Mormon converts to America. Many of these converts came from the poorer classes. They were ready to forsake their poverty for the better life promised in 'Zion'. Between 1840 and 1890 55,000 of them emigrated. Those who survived the hardships of the sea voyage and the long treks that followed it, certainly made their impact. 'These English emigrants and their descendants contributed at least 50 per cent and possibly 70 per cent of the Church's leadership in the years since.'[13] 'The Church in America became predominantly English for the next fifty years.'[14]

Back in America, Young's powers of leadership were put to the test when Smith and other prominent Mormons were arrested in Missouri. It was left to Young to plan the mass Mormon evacuation from that state. After Smith's murder in 1844, Young assumed the Church's leadership and three years later he was officially recognised as the movement's new President, Prophet, Seer and Revelator.

The Great Trek

Brigham Young is best remembered for his leadership of the historic trek to the West of America. The exodus began in 1846, following continuous persecution. It quickly gained momentum. 'It is estimated that before the railroad came in 1869, about 80,000 Mormon pioneers travelled this 1,000 mile distance, some in covered wagons drawn by mules and oxen; some pushing their possessions in handcarts; and some walking all the way. About 6,000 lost their lives and lie buried in unmarked graves between the Missouri river and the western slopes of the Rocky Mountains.'[15]

Although he organised the trek on strict military lines, Young came to be regarded, not merely as a general leading an army, but as a latter-day Moses leading a new Israel to its promised land. Those who safely reached their destination built Salt Lake City, the Mormon headquarters ever since, and founded what was to become the State of Utah. When he died in 1877, he left behind him a strongly bureaucratic structure which has provided the Mormon Church's governing framework ever since.

CONSOLIDATION AND PROGRESS

Polygamy Outlawed

Young was succeeded by John Taylor, who had been severely wounded at Smith's side when the Mormon founder was murdered. His presidency coincided with a determined effort by the United States Government to stamp out polygamy. The 1882 Edmunds Bill deprived polygamists of the right to vote, to hold public office, or to serve on a jury. The 1887 Edmunds-Tucker Bill intensified the pressure. It dissolved the Church as a corporate body, seized its property, and disinherited the children of plural marriages. Taylor's successor, Wilford Woodruff, made Mormonism's peace with the Federal Government. His 'Official Declaration' of 1890 instructed Mormons to give up polygamy and submit to the law of the land. The Government then declared an amnesty for all Mormon polygamists, restored the Church's property, and granted Utah statehood in 1896.

Small pockets of fundamentalist Mormons still practise polygamy. They argue that they are being consistent to the belief that a divine revelation once given through the Mormon prophet cannot be rescinded because it does not suit an earthly government. Invariably, they are excommunicated by the Mormon Church and also come into conflict with the secular authorities. Even the mainstream Mormons, who do not now practise polygamy, expect it to be reintroduced at some future time, probably during the millennium but, if not then, certainly in the next life.

The Twentieth Century

The next fifty years saw four Mormon presidents and a significant growth in the movement's world-wide membership. Then came David McKay, who led the movement from 1951 to 1970. After Joseph Smith and Brigham Young, he did as much for Mormonism as any other leader. He carried through a widespread education and training programme, increased missionary activity, and approved the building of six new Mormon temples, including the British temple near Lingfield, Surrey, in 1958. Ezra Taft Benson became the Mormon leader in November 1985 at the age of 86, after being an apostle since 1943. He has a distinguished political pedigree, having served as a member of President Eisenhower's cabinet.

WHAT MORMONS BELIEVE

Revelation

As we have seen, the fundamental Mormon belief, from which all their other doctrines stem, is that, just as in former times God revealed his truth partially through other agents, so now in these latter-days he has revealed the fullness of his Gospel truth through Joseph Smith. Mormons regard Smith's books, *The Book of Mormon, Doctrine and*

Covenants, and *Pearl of Great Price*, as the Word of God. Alongside the Bible, they are the governing scriptures of the Mormon Church. All that is distinctive in Mormon teaching comes from these three Mormon books and generally deviates considerably from mainstream Christianity.

God

Although Mormon writers often use traditional Christian language, they use it to mean something other than what it means to mainstream Christians. This is particularly true of the Mormon view of God.

Mormons believe that God is **tangible**. Arguing from Genesis 1.26–27 that man is made in God's image, they maintain that God is like man and must have a physical body of flesh and bones as real as any other male body, claiming that Deuteronomy 4.28 also supports this view. Mormon writer Le Grand Richards, for example, claimed that the true God, as contrasted with the idols mentioned in Deuteronomy, could see, hear, eat and smell, and must, therefore, possess a physical body with the organs enabling him to do these things.[16] Some Mormons have gone further, maintaining that their 'god with a physical body' probably has a physical relationship with a female divine being. They have been reticent in discussing this with non-Mormons, but it seems a logical, if, from a Christian standpoint, a blasphemous, development of their doctrine of God's tangibility.

Despite the Mormon claim to find support for God's tangibility in Deuteronomy, Christians and Jews would see the passage forbidding the making of idols on the grounds that, when God spoke to Israel, the people heard his voice but saw no form. 'On the day when the Lord spoke to you out of the fire on Horeb, you saw no figure of any kind; so take care not to fall into the degrading practice of making figures carved in relief, in the form of a man or a woman, or of an animal on earth or bird that flies in the air, or of any reptile on the ground or fish in the waters under the earth.'[17] They would therefore regard this passage as strong evidence against the view that God has a physical form. The real basis of this Mormon belief, however, is not the Bible, but Smith's first vision in which he claimed to see the Father and the Son in physical form. Clearly here, as in many other cases, Joseph Smith and the Bible part company.

The idea of an **evolving** God is also an integral part of Mormon theology. The Supreme God is, as it were, at the top of a moving escalator, whilst most of the rest of us have stepped on at the bottom. Even God has not always been at the top, however, having ascended from a more lowly position. As Smith himself used to say, 'God himself was once as we are now, and is an exalted man'. It remains an important maxim of Mormon teaching that, 'As man is, God once was; as God is, man may become'. This means that the difference between God and human beings is simply a difference of degree. He has reached the top of the escalator before the rest of us.

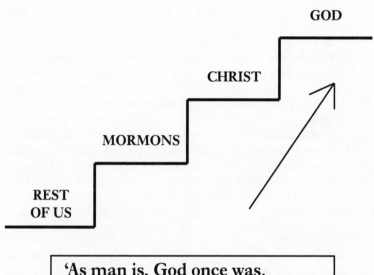

'As man is, God once was.
As God is, man may become'.

Older Mormon writers spoke openly of a **plurality** of gods, a Council of the Gods over whom the Supreme God presides. As well as Jesus Christ, this Council included Enoch, Elijah, Abraham, Peter, and Paul. Smith told his followers, 'You have got to learn how to be Gods yourselves ... the same as all Gods have done before you, namely by going from one small degree to another.' It was such teaching that led one non-Mormon writer to conclude that Mormonism was 'polytheistic to the core'.[18] Such views are completely repudiated by such passages as Exodus 20.1-6, Isaiah 40.12-31, and Isaiah 45.18, which all stress that the Lord God is the one, sovereign and eternal God, besides whom there is no other God.

Contemporary Mormons are more cautious, pointing out that they distinguish between these 'gods' and the trinity of Father, Son and Holy Ghost. Even when speaking of the trinity, however, the views expressed are very different from the view of the trinity held by mainstream Christians. Mormons come close to thinking of Father, Son and Holy Ghost, not as three Persons within the unity of the Godhead, but of three separate gods.

Jesus Christ

The Mormon view of Christ has to be seen against the background of their doctrines of God and the pre-existence of human spirits. Mormons believe that our pre-existent spirits were all 'begotten of Heavenly Parents even as Jesus was'. The implications are clear. Either Christ is a creature like us, or we are part of the Godhead like him. In either case the essential uniqueness of Christ, as taught in the Bible and upheld by Christian tradition, disappears altogether. He is little different from the rest of us. Like his Father, he is simply further up the escalator. Seen in this light, the traditional language used in Mormonism is emptied of its meaning.

The Holy Spirit

Mormons try to distinguish between the Holy Ghost, whom they are happy to describe as the third personage of the Godhead, on the one hand, and the Spirit of God or of Jesus, on the other. They say the Holy Ghost works only in those who are baptised as Mormons and have received the laying-on of hands of the Mormon priesthood. The Spirit of God or of Christ, in contrast, is 'the medium through which God controls the universe and by which he may inspire and direct his children'. Though often 'likened to the light of the sun, to electricity, or to the electrons of which all matter and life are composed, it has not been identified with any one of them and may be a substance unknown to man aside from his spiritual experience with it.'[19] It enlightens every person coming into the world.

Salvation

'Not one of our Father's children is born in spiritual darkness', state the Mormons. 'Little children are alive in Christ even from the foundation of the world.'[20] They go on to assert that our very presence in the world is an indication that in our previous spiritual existence we proved ourselves worthy to be born. Life on earth, therefore, is a second probationary period. Those who pass this test successfully will progress towards godhood.

Mormons, however, believe that there are different grades of salvation, or exaltation (as they prefer to call it). 'These are designated as the celestial, or highest, the terrestrial, and the telestial. The difference between these conditions has been likened to the difference in brilliance of the sun, the moon, and stars as viewed from this planet. Within each glory there are again numerous divisions or gradations according to the worthiness of the individuals who enter therein.'[21]

They find biblical justification for this view in 1 Corinthians 15, in which Paul speaks of a glory of the sun, a glory of the moon, and a glory of the stars. With the same basic misunderstanding of the passage, one could proceed to argue for 'animal glory, 'bird glory', and 'fish glory', for Paul also mentions these in that chapter. Many commentators would regard this as missing the whole point of the apostle's argument, for in his teaching about the resurrection, he is stating that every form of life has a 'body' appropriate to its environment. So, too, he concludes, in the resurrected state we who on earth have 'physical bodies' will then have 'spiritual bodies', that is, bodies appropriate to a heavenly environment. An illustration from natural science is provided by the caterpillar and the butterfly, the different kinds of life requiring two different kinds of body.

Baptism

Baptism has such an important place in the Mormon scheme of salvation that Mormons are expected to be baptised by immersion not only once for themselves but also on other occasions vicariously for their dead relatives so that they too may be given a chance to be saved. That is why Mormons are so deeply committed to genealogical research. The more obedient a Mormon becomes in being baptised for the dead, the more he or she increases the level of personal salvation.

Faith and Works

The Mormon answer to the age-old question, 'What must I do to be saved?', therefore, turns out to be: repent, have faith, be baptised for yourself and for others, receive the laying-on of hands, and seal your marriage for eternity. **Repentance** includes the giving up of tea, coffee and alcohol, as well as turning from moral evil. **Faith** seems to be more the acceptance of the long list of Mormon ordinances rather than personal trust in Christ bringing forgiveness, new life, and a restored relationship with God as Father. **The laying-on of hands**, the Mormon equivalent of confirmation in some mainstream Christian churches, is the Mormon method of receiving the Holy Ghost. **Celestial marriage**, through which the marriage covenant between a couple is sealed for eternity, is essential for those wishing to achieve the highest level of salvation. The Mormon formula for salvation becomes, therefore, a kind of mathematical sum. The more plusses, the higher the grade!

The Work of Christ

Where does Christ fit into this scheme? In places Mormon writers seem to be expressing orthodox Christian views. Le Grand Richards, for example, writes that Christ 'redeemed us from the fall; he paid the price; he offered himself as a ransom'. A little later, however, he completely repudiates the doctrine of justification by grace through faith. 'Christ atoned for Adam's sin, leaving us responsible for our own sins ... We free ourselves from the consequences of a broken law, and entitle ourselves to the blessings predicated upon obedience to divine law ... Hence, as we continue our quest to know and understand the laws of God, and obey them, we increase the measure of our salvation or exaltation.'[22] What he appears to be arguing is that Christ died to free us from the consequences of Adam's sin (i.e. physical death), leaving us free to work for our own salvation.

The Future

Mormons believe that there will be a two-fold gathering process before Christ returns to the earth to reign for a thousand years. First, the Latter-day Saints will be gathered into an American Zion. Secondly, the Jews will be gathered around Jerusalem.

During the millennium, Mormons will engage in a threefold task: building temples, baptising for the dead, and preaching the Mormon gospel. The preaching will be directed to those who, though not Mormons, have been considered worthy enough to remain on earth during this period. All who live on during the thousand years will reach the age of a hundred and will then be suddenly changed to immortality. The wicked, though dead physically, will survive spiritually, and will be given another chance to repent and purify themselves through suffering.

At the end of the millennium all will be raised and judged. A renewed earth will then become the abode of those found worthy of the highest grade of salvation. The remainder of the human race will be housed elsewhere. The damned, that is a third of the spirit world who rebelled before the world was made and a fairly small number of human beings guilty of the worst sins and beyond the possibility of repentance and salvation, will spend eternity in hell.

WHERE MORMONS AND MAINSTREAM CHRISTIANS PART COMPANY

MORMONS	CHRISTIANS

The Bible

A partial and inadequate record of God's revelation. *The Book of Mormon, Doctrine and Covenants* and *Pearl of Great Price* are also God's Word. God continues to reveal his will through the Mormon priesthood, and especially through the Mormon president who is regarded as a prophet.	God has revealed all that he wants us to know of himself and his will for us in Christ, his incarnate Word and what we know of Christ is contained in the Bible, his written word. The Bible is the norm by which all claims to religious truth are to be measured, including those claiming a prophetic gift.

God

God the Father (like his Son) has a physical male body, evolved to his divine status from manhood, and could be one of a plurality of similar divine beings.	God is Father, Son and Holy Spirit, three Persons within the unity of the Godhead. God is Creator, we are his creatures. The difference between God and us is one of nature, not merely of degree.

MORMONS	CHRISTIANS
Christ	
Christ is God's Son and a divine being. Like his Father, he has a physical body. He also differs from human beings in the degree to which he has progressed along the spectrum from manhood to Godhead.	Christ is the eternal Son of the Father. He became incarnate, taking up our humanity into his Godhood, for our salvation. In his unique Person, the divine and the human natures are united.
The Holy Spirit	
The Holy Ghost is a divine Person but unlike the Father and the Son has no physical body. Mormons distinguish between the Holy Ghost and the Spirit of God or of Jesus. The Holy Ghost appears to work only in Mormons, whereas the Spirit of God or of Jesus works throughout the universe.	The Holy Spirit, the Spirit of God and the Spirit of Jesus are different titles for the one Spirit. As God in action, the one divine Spirit is at work in individuals, in the Church, and in the world, inspiring and enabling people to do God's will.
Salvation	
With the exception of a few very wicked people, and a third of the angels who fell before the world was created, all will be exalted (saved). Christ frees us from the consequences of Adam's sin, leaving us responsible for our own sin. Salvation is through obedience to the Mormon ordinances, such as baptism for yourself and vicarious baptism for dead relatives, the laying-on of hands, and the celestial marriage which binds couples for eternity. Salvation is graded according to the level of obedience given by the individual concerned.	Achieved by Christ, who died on the cross and rose again for us, salvation is not something we earn by obedience or in any other way, but is God's gracious gift which is appropriated through trusting in Christ as Saviour. The same full salvation, or wholeness, is offered to all in Christ. It does not depend upon our level of obedience: we obey God, not to achieve salvation, but because we love him for what he has done for us in Christ.

MORMONS	CHRISTIANS

The Church

| The Mormon Church, that is the Church of Jesus Christ of Latter-day Saints, is the restored Church and therefore the only true Church and its priests are the only legitimate priests of God. All other so-called Churches are apostate and their ministers are impostors. | The one true Church is that founded on the apostles and prophets, with Christ as the chief cornerstone. It consists of all who have accepted Christ as Saviour and acknowledge him as Lord. The whole Church is a holy priesthood, though within its membership some are called (and often ordained) to specific roles of leadership. |

The Future

| Zion will be established in America, the Jews will be gathered around Jerusalem, and Christ will return. During the ensuing millennium, Mormon missionary work will continue. The day of judgement will follow. | The whole of history will reach its climax and the Kingdom of God will come in all its fullness when Christ comes again in glory. The faithful will then enjoy God's presence eternally. |

THE MORMON CHURCH AND ITS ORGANISATION

The Church

Like many sects, Mormons claim that they alone have God's truth in its fullness. This view is seen particularly in their assertions about the Church. The Mormon Church is the only true Church. One of their publications states: 'Alone among Christian denominations, it includes important and distinctive teachings ... The most central of these is the conviction that the church which Christ himself established while on earth did not long survive the death of the apostles. A succession of changes, unauthorised by scripture or by divine revelation, was introduced into the early church in the first few centuries after Christ.' Among the changes enumerated are the introduction of formalism into worship, radical changes in the concept of deity, the introduction of infant baptism, and alterations in church organisation 'including the elevation of the status of the bishop of Rome'. The document continues, 'These were not cosmetic changes, but fundamental alterations to the faith which Christ taught. These and other developments – well documented in history – drove the Church into total apostasy'.[23] The Mormon Church founded by Smith in 1830, therefore, is now the only legitimate successor to the Church founded by Christ.

Without in any way wishing to deny the faults and failings of the Christian Church through the centuries, it is clear that the Mormon view requires a completely arbitrary re-writing of Church history. The idea that the Church as such ceased to exist on earth between about AD 70 and 1830 really does take some swallowing!

The Mormon Priesthood

Mormonism is a male-dominated organisation, a priesthood in which almost every male Mormon plays a part. Following the pattern established in 1830 by Joseph Smith, this priesthood has two main divisions.

The Aaronic or Levitical Priesthood, made up of deacons, teachers and priests, is the lesser priesthood. A Mormon boy becomes a deacon when he is twelve, a teacher at fourteen, and a priest at sixteen.

The Melchizedek Priesthood is for male Mormons aged nineteen and over. It is made up of elders, seventies, and high priests. It is the superior and more powerful part of the Mormon organisation. Elders have a mainly local role; seventies are travelling ministers, usually of middle age, who may be called by the Mormon Church to do missionary work anywhere in the world; and high priests occupy all the key positions in the hierarchy.

Until 1978 black people, like women today, were barred from the priesthood. On 9th June that year, however, the President announced that 'all worthy male members of the Church may be ordained to the priesthood without regard for race or colour'. This change of policy was justified on the grounds that it had been indicated in another God-given revelation to the Mormon Church through its President. The truth appears to be that once more (as previously over the question of polygamy) Mormons have yielded to the mounting pressure of public opinion. Perhaps in time women will also become eligible for ordination to the priesthood.

General Authorities

At the apex of the priestly hierarchy, directing all the Church's affairs, is **the First Presidency**. This is a powerful triumvirate consisting of the president and his two counsellors. All authority exercised within Mormonism is regarded as authority delegated from this First Presidency and, therefore, from God. It ensures the continuance of traditional Mormon beliefs and practices and makes all the Church's senior appointments.

The Mormon president continues to be described as President, Prophet, Seer, and Revelator. He is still believed to be the mouthpiece of God, the agent through whom divine revelations are given to God's people. In practice, however, such revelations are not accepted as God's word until they have received the approval of the Mormon Church's general conference. Even then they are not now added to *Doctrine and Covenants*.

Next comes **the Quorum of the Twelve Apostles**. Their special task is to 'build up and organise the branches of the Church' and to 'travel among the Saints, regulating the affairs of the Church wherever they go'.[24]

The First Quorum of Seventy is the next stage down the hierarchical ladder. Their task is to administer the work of the Mormon Church around the globe. A member of this quorum, for example, supervises Mormon work in the British Isles.

These General Authorities, some sixty key men, are Mormonism's top leadership. They have authority throughout the Church as the chief policy-formers and decision-makers. Unlike other Mormon officials, these all serve the Mormon Church in a full-time capacity. Under them the Mormon bureaucracy is divided territorially into Stakes and Wards, Missions and Branches.

Stakes and Wards

A Mormon **stake** corresponds roughly to an English diocese, whilst a ward is a smaller unit comparable to a local church congregation. The number of wards in a stake varies from place to place, being determined by such factors as geographical convenience and the density of the local Mormon population. The stake's chief officer is the stake president, who must be a high priest and who is assisted by two other high priests acting as his counsellors.

Each Mormon **ward** has its bishop and his two counsellors who together lead the local Mormon congregation. A ward may have around

400 members and a stake, which may be responsible for up to eight wards, up to 4,000 members. Where the number of local Mormons is too small to warrant the formation of stakes and wards, a district is formed and this is in turn subdivided into branches.

Regional Authorities

With the growth of Mormonism throughout the world, the Church has divided its work into some 256 regions. These are supervised by regional representatives of the Twelve Apostles. Regions are composed of groups of stakes. The regional representatives are responsible for the training of stake presidents, co-ordinating stake activities, and generally supervising the work of the Church in their geographical area.

As the following diagram shows, the Church of Jesus Christ of Latter-day Saints is a carefully controlled bureaucracy with an organisation comparable to the management structures of some large business corporations. It appears to work very well.

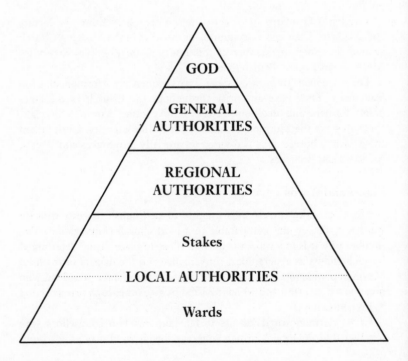

THE MORMON CHURCH'S OUTREACH

Mormon Missionaries

The most probable contact non-Mormons will have with Mormonism is through Mormon missionaries. Nearly 30,000 of them, mostly men between the ages of nineteen and twenty-two, work in ninety countries, using literature translated into seventy languages. About 1,600 of them are based in the British Isles, 200 in each of the eight mission areas into which Mormons have divided it.

All missionaries are unpaid, being supported by their families and friends and their own savings. Working in pairs, they may spend as much as six to eight hours visiting in a day. With this first visit, they try to gain entrance to the home. They focus their efforts chiefly on families, where possible. Subsequent visits aim to explain Mormon teaching, assisted by a whole range of audio-visual resources, including videos. In some developing countries Mormon missionaries have a health and welfare role. The overriding aim of all missionaries, however, is to convince their contacts of the truth of the Mormon claims and to make them members of the Mormon Church.

Mormon Chapels

Multi-purpose Mormon chapels play an important part in this outreach. They are used for social and recreational activities, as well as for worship. The best of them provide a wide range of resources, including a suite of purpose-built classrooms, library and other educational facilities, and a cultural hall for sports, drama, music and dance activities. Thirty three of the British chapels also provide facilities for genealogical research. Mormons claim that the non-Mormon to Mormon ratio of usage of this particular facility is ten to one. To the Mormons themselves, however, the genealogical research has a particular significance, because of their practice of baptism for the dead.

Mormon Families

Great emphasis is placed on the importance of family life, for Mormons regard it as the basic unit of their work. One evening a week (often Monday) is set aside as a special 'Family Home Evening', when members are encouraged to spend time together in spiritual and recreational activities designed to build good relationships and strong family ties. Because they regard the family as an eternal unit, members of Mormon families are 'sealed together, not just for this life, but for all eternity' through temple ceremonies such as proxy baptism and celestial marriage.[25]

The Mormon Welfare programme

The Mormon Church has an extensive and well-organised welfare programme, and spends many thousands of dollars assisting an average of about 100,000 people each year. In what is known as a 'fast offering', all members are expected to abstain from food and drink for two meals on the first Sunday of each month, which is known as 'Fast Sunday'. The money thus saved is given to the local Mormon bishop to provide for the Mormon poor and needy.

On a more general scale, 'the storehouse resource system' provides an increasing number of storehouses, wherever Mormon membership in a particular area makes this practicable. Food, clothing, and other supplies are kept in readiness for Mormons who fall on hard times. The British storehouse is in Birmingham.

The local Mormon bishop fulfils an important role in the administration of the welfare programme. In addition to his oversight of the ward's worship, teaching and social activities, he is expected to ensure that none of his members wants for the necessities of life. He is supported by the ward's Relief Society, a women's meeting. Its president shares with him the oversight of a network of visitors, who call on members monthly to minister to their spiritual and temporal needs.

To help to resource this kind of programme, in recent years the Mormon Church has been buying up significant quantities of agricultural land in Britain.

Mormon Tithing

There is little shortage of money in the Mormon Church, for members are expected to give a tenth of their gross income to the Church's work. Apart from the full-time general authorities of the Church, all officials are unpaid. Most of the income is directed towards missionary work and chapel building. News releases from the Mormon Church have stated that in recent years considerable sums of money have been spent acquiring good agricultural land in Britain to support the Mormon welfare programme. In the United States of America Mormon outreach is resourced by the Church's involvement in a variety of business operations.

REFERENCES

1. Gospel Ideal, p.98.
2. A. Hoekema, *The Four Major Cults*, Paternoster 1969, p.84.
3. Le Grand Richards, *A Marvelous Work and a Wonder*, Deseret Book Company 1956, p.1.
4. *Doctrine and Covenants* 2:1.
5. *Doctrine and Covenants* 21:5.
6. Fawn Brodie, *No Man Knows My History*, Knopf 1971, page 397.
7. Cited W.R. Martin, *The Maze of Mormonism*, Zondervan 1962, pp.23f.
8. Fawn Brodie, op. cit. page 84.
9. Martin, op cit, p.46.
10. Cited Martin, ibid.
11. *The Book of Mormon*, 1 Nephi 11:13ff and 2 Nephi 2:6ff.
12. Thomas O'Dea, *The Mormons*, p.13.
13. R. Mullen, *The Mormons*, W.H. Allen 1967, p.65.
14. W. Berrett, *The Restored Church*, Deseret Book Company 1965, p.153 (Like many American writers, Berrett means 'British' when he writes 'English').
15. *Encyclopaedia Britannica*.
16. Le Grand Richards, op cit, p.14.
17. Deuteronomy 4:15-18.
18. Martin, op cit, p.81.
19. Berrett, op cit, page 389.
20. Le Grand Richards, op cit, p.100.
21. Berrett, op cit, p.413.
22. Le Grand Richards, op cit, pp.279ff.
23. *Mormon Media Pack 1*.
24. J.E. Talmage, *Articles of Faith*, Mormon Church 1908, p.212
25. *Mormon Media Pack 5*

Chapter 2
JEHOVAH'S WITNESSES

During the past ten years, I have been visited by Jehovah's Witnesses at least thirty times. My experience is not exceptional. Of all the sects at work in Britain today, Jehovah's Witnesses are the most persistent in their door-to-door work. They keep careful statistics of their membership and of their activities. According to their own published figures for 1994, each of their 4,914,094 members devoted an average of about 224 hours to this work during that year, that is about 4.3 hours a week each. The 1995 *Yearbook* of Jehovah's Witnesses lists some 232 countries in which the movement is working and claims that in 1994 a total of 314,818 new converts were baptised.

The 1995 *Yearbook* distinguishes between 'publishers' and those who attend the annual 'Memorial Service'. For many years the movement has recognised as members only those who actively serve as publishers, a 1994 peak of 4,914,094. From the number of Memorial Service attenders, however, it seems reasonable to conclude that world-wide the movement attracts the support of over 12.3 million people, about 40 per cent of whom are actively engaged in door-to-door work.

Jehovah's Witnesses are particularly active in the United States of America, where there are nearly 2 million attenders of whom 936,264 (47 per cent) are publishers. Mexico has 1.4 million attenders of whom 404,593 are publishers and Brazil one million attenders of whom 385,099 are publishers. Nigeria, the Philippines, Zambia, Japan and Italy boast between 350,000 to 500,000 attenders each, with roughly a 40 per cent as active publishers. Germany has 291,717 attenders of whom 167,878 (57.5 per cent) are publishers, France 238,445 attenders of whom 123,718 (51.9 per cent) are publishers, whilst the numbers for Britain are 226,298 attenders of whom 129,852 (57.4 per cent) are active publishers. If these figures are accurate, they show that a very high proportion of those who attend Jehovah's Witness functions are active in the movement's door-to-door work.

But who are these Jehovah's Witnesses? How did they originate? What methods do they use to spread their teaching? What do they believe? How different are they from mainstream Christians? These are some of the questions we need to consider in the rest of this chapter.

We begin with a little history.

CHARLES TAZE RUSSELL

Jehovah's Witnesses have a less dramatic history than Mormons. There is no unique story to compare with that of Joseph Smith's visions and plates, no epic journey like that of Bringham Young and the other Mormon founders of Salt Lake City and Utah. There is no specific Jehovah's Witness 'revelation', no enduring 'myth'. The only thing that Charles Russell, the sect's founder, claimed was that he faithfully represented the teaching of the Bible, which he believed to be the Word of God. His argument with mainstream Christianity was that the churches had distorted, misrepresented, ignored and rejected the Bible. Subsequent leaders of the sect have made the same claims. In that sense, therefore, Jehovah's Witnesses are a 'Bible-only sect', in contrast to people like Mormons and Christian Scientists, who are 'Bible-plus sects'.

Nevertheless, the history of Jehovah's Witnesses ought not to be ignored. It is essential for those wishing to understand why Jehovah's Witnesses believe what they believe and act as they do.

Charles Taze Russell was born on 16th February 1852 in Pittsburgh, Pennsylvania. Following his mother's death when he was only nine, Russell developed a close relationship with his father and later joined him in a clothing business. A seriously minded young man, Russell's upbringing followed a Presbyterian-Congregationalist pattern. For a time he was a member of the Young Men's Christian Association. He showed some evangelistic zeal as an adolescent: when only fifteen he used to chalk texts on walls so that passing workmen might be reminded of their need to repent.

At this stage, Russell's Christianity was fairly orthodox. Soon, however, he began to have serious doubts about Christian belief. He turned to Oriental religions hoping to find them more satisfying. When he was at the point of giving up religion completely, he heard a sermon by an Adventist preacher, Jonas Wendell, and was convinced of the divine inspiration of the Bible. From that day onwards, Russell was an ardent Bible student.

Rejection of Mainstream Christianity

Claiming to approach the Bible without any preconceived ideas, Russell decided that many of the tenets of orthodox Christianity were unscriptural and ought to be rejected. He also came to believe, with many of the Adventists of the time, that a literal second coming of Christ was imminent. From 1870 to 1875 he and five other like-minded people used to meet for Bible study. The sect's official history describes this as a time of 'unlearning many cherished errors'.[1] Among the beliefs then discarded were some of the cardinal doctrines of the Christian faith, including that of the trinity.

The Second Presence

Russell soon disagreed with the Adventists, with whom he had at first appeared to have much in common. He rejected the view that Christ was about to return in visible form, replacing it with the view that he would return invisibly. He publicised this idea in a pamphlet, *The Object and Manner of the Lord's Return*, some 50,000 copies of which were distributed by his small band of supporters.

By 1876 Russell had made about thirty disciples. He then met N.H. Barbour, author of a magazine called *The Herald of the Morning*, with whose views he was pleased to discover he had much in common. In particular they both shared the belief in an invisible Second Coming. They found support for this view in the Diaglott translation of the New Testament by a Christadelphian named Benjamin Wilson, in which the Greek *parousia* had been translated 'presence' instead of 'coming'. For a time the two men joined forces. Russell became co-editor of Barbour's magazine. Russell had already given up his clothing business to devote his life to full-time preaching. He used to travel from city to city, preaching on weekdays in the open air and on Sundays in Protestant churches.

He and Barbour wrote *Three Worlds, or Plan of Redemption*, in which they argued that Christ's second presence, as they were now calling it, had begun in the autumn of 1874. They went on to claim that, just as at his first coming Christ had preached for three and a half years, so his second presence would be of a similar duration. This meant that God's kingdom would be set up in 1878 and that the saints on earth would then be carried away into heaven.

Anticipating that event, some of their followers dressed themselves in white robes and assembled to await their expected rapture. Subsequent disillusionment led them to forsake Russell and Barbour. Russell, however, merely went back to his study of the Bible, concluding that the mistake had been the result of a miscalculation. Such miscalculations have been characteristic of Jehovah's Witnesses ever since. For example, Jehovah's Witnesses were expecting the world to end in 1975.

The Watchtower Magazine

Following doctrinal disagreements, Russell and Barbour parted company in 1879 and Russell then started his own magazine, *The Watch Tower and Herald of Christ's Presence*. Now known by the shorter name *The Watchtower*, it has a circulation of many millions each fortnightly issue and appears in about a hundred languages. It is the movement's official mouthpiece.

Within a year of the magazine's appearance, Russell's growing number of supporters were organised in thirty congregations in Pennsylvania and the surrounding states. They found their unity, not in the elaborate bureaucratic structure which developed later, but in a common informal acceptance of Russell's leadership and in a willingness to follow the pattern set by the Pittsburgh congregation, where Russell himself was pastor.

The Watch Tower Bible and Tract Society

These early Russellites, as they were known, busied themselves in producing and distributing many tracts. Their aim was to 'expose fallacies of church doctrines'. To help them to achieve that aim, Russell established Zion's Watch Tower Tract Society in 1881. It had seven directors, including a president (Russell), a vice-president, and a secretary-treasurer. There was a change of name in 1896 to the present Watch Tower Bible and Tract Society, but the earlier leadership pattern of seven directors has remained.

The number of Russell's followers increased steadily as the years went by, largely because of his own ceaseless activities. After the success of *The Watchtower*, he produced many books. Among the most important were his *Studies in the Scriptures*, which set out clearly his own distinctive and controversial views, and which his followers came to regard as indispensable for understanding the Bible.

Russell also travelled widely, preaching, lecturing and promoting his writings. He visited Great Britain four times. The London branch office was opened in 1900 and the International Bible Students' Association, an offshoot of the American Watch Tower Society, was founded there in 1914.

Marriage and Divorce

In 1879 Russell had married Maria Frances Ackley. For seventeen years Mrs Russell fully supported her husband's religious activities, speaking and writing to further the sect's work. After a disagreement over editorial policy, however, the two separated and were eventually divorced. Opponents have tried to make capital out of Russell's marital problems, and there is some evidence that his relations with the opposite sex were not always discreet. There is little evidence, however, of the immorality and cruelty of which he has often been accused. It seems that the marriage eventually broke up because of the Russells' incompatibility.

The End

After the 1878 disappointment, when the faithful were not taken up to heaven, Russell went on to predict that the Christ who had returned invisibly in 1874 would take the elect into God's kingdom in 1914. Excitement mounted as the year approached, with the Russellites working feverishly to prepare people for the expected end. Millions of publications were distributed and Russell's sermons were syndicated in newspapers across North America and Europe. Membership grew to 15,000, with 55,000 regular subscribers to *The Watchtower*.

Russell became less explicit as 1914 drew near. In contrast, many of his followers continued to make extravagant claims, bringing ridicule upon themselves and the movement. The year ended in disappointment, with the promised rapture unfulfilled. As it happened, Russell's own end was not long delayed, for on 31st October 1916 he died in Texas, returning from a preaching tour.

Jehovah's Witnesses claim that their founder travelled more than a million miles, preached more than 30,000 sermons, and wrote books totalling over 50,000 pages.[2] Though holding him in high regard, his Society has never published his biography, fearing that it might give to a man the credit which belongs to God. *The Watchtower* of 1st May 1917 was not so inhibited, claiming, 'Not since the Apostle Paul has there lived a greater and better man than Pastor Russell'.

J.F. RUTHERFORD

After a brief but bitter struggle for power, J.F. Rutherford emerged as the sect's new leader. Born in Missouri on 8th November 1869, he became a successful lawyer and eventually a circuit judge in his home state. He came into contact with Russell's teaching in 1894 through the work of a door-to-door visitor, but was not baptised until 1906. His rise within the movement was rapid. He became Russell's legal advisor in 1907 and was employed at the sect's Pittsburgh headquarters. As Russell's health began to decline, Rutherford came into prominence as an able speaker, sometimes substituting for his sick leader. Ten years after joining the movement he became its leader.

Change of Style

His style was very different from the gentler Russell's and this led to inevitable conflict with those who had previously worked closely with the founder. Rutherford, however, proved more than a match for his opponents. A few disaffected members formed small, breakaway groups, some of which persisted, but Rutherford retained the loyalty of most members. He was to prove an able leader.

It is instructive to notice the steps he took to ensure his personal control over every aspect of the movement's activities. They not only reveal facets of his character, but also help us to understand some of the characteristics that persist in the movement to this day.

Rutherford's overall aim was to tighten up the sect's rather loose organisation, to rid it of all democratic elements, and to transform it into a tightly knit bureaucratic structure over which he reigned supreme. He explained that democracy must give way to theocracy, human control to divine control. He quickly got rid of those directors who were not willing to back him and all members of the headquarters staff who sympathised with their views.

Congregational Control

Next he turned his attention to the congregations. Under Russell, these had been linked together in a loose fellowship. In place of their democratically elected leaders, he insisted that the most important work, that of door-to-door outreach and literature distribution, must be placed under the direct control of congregation service directors whom he appointed. By 1932 these service directors had completely ousted the former elders and had total control of the congregations. Six years later the last vestiges of democracy were completely removed, with Rutherford insisting that all congregation office holders were to be appointed by the Society. Earlier he had introduced the zone system, with a number of congregations being grouped together in a geographical area and made accountable to a zone servant, who was himself accountable to Rutherford. In such ways Rutherford succeeded in imposing his own bureaucratic structure upon the movement. Over it all, he exercised almost absolute power.

Doctrinal Uniformity

One of Rutherford's earliest problems was the posthumous influence over the movement of his former leader. He gradually replaced all Russell's publications with his own. Books like *The Harp of God*, *Jehovah*, *Creation*, and *Life*, ensured that Rutherford, rather than his predecessor, became the sect's arbiter in all matters of faith and conduct.

His concern for doctrinal uniformity led him in 1922 to order that future study of *The Watchtower* should be done in groups as well as individually, and that members should answer printed questions on the magazine's articles to ensure that they had imbibed its teaching. Rutherford also ensured uniformity of presentation of the sect's teachings to those outside the movement by producing a monthly Bulletin containing talks and testimonies for use in outreach.

Imprisonment

The First World War proved a difficult time for Rutherford and his followers. Because of the sect's view that its members should not fight for any earthly power, its publications were regarded as seditious. This was especially true in the United States where the Army Intelligence Bureau began to investigate the Society's New York headquarters. Matters came to a head on 7th May 1918 when Rutherford and seven other members were charged with 'unlawfully, feloniously, and wilfully causing insubordination, disloyalty and refusal of duty in the military and naval forces of the United States of America', and were sentenced to long terms of imprisonment. Rutherford and those arrested with him were released on bail pending an appeal. With the ending of the war, they were cleared of all charges. But for the hysteria of the war years, it is likely that none of them would have been arrested in the first place. As it happened, however, his period in prison enhanced Rutherford's reputation, for his followers saw him as a man prepared to suffer for what he believed.

A New Name

The movement owes its name to Rutherford. In 1925 he told his followers that 'Jehovah' was the proper name for God. Six years later he renamed his followers 'Jehovah's Witnesses', thus bringing to an end the confusion which had arisen from the various other names by which they had been known previously, such as Russellites, Millennial Dawnists, Footstep Followers of Jesus, and International Bible Students. Another change came in 1935, when Jehovah's Witnesses began to call their meeting places 'Kingdom Halls', a practice which is now universal among Witnesses.

Rutherford's Death

Rutherford died on 8th January 1942 after an illness which had made him increasingly less active in the movement's affairs. He had inherited from Russell a number of democratic, autonomous groups, in a loose federation based on a common loyalty to Russell. He had transformed these congregations into a tightly knit, centrally controlled, 'theocratic' organisation, over which he held supreme power. During his presidency, membership had increased from 16,000 to more than 100,000.

THE WATCH TOWER SOCIETY

The personality-cult associated with the movement's first two leaders has been played down during the last fifty years. Nathan H. Knorr, who followed Rutherford, though lacking the personal appeal of his predecessors, proved a very effective leader.

The Watch Tower Translation of the Bible

One of the most important events of his presidency was the publication of The New World Translation of the Bible. Jehovah's Witnesses prefer it to any other version, claiming that, unlike all other translations, this one is not coloured in any way by the doctrinal presuppositions of those responsible for it. It would appear that almost the exact opposite is true, for at many points The New World Translation translates the text so that it supports specific Jehovah's Witness doctrines.

The Hierarchy

Whereas both Russell and Rutherford kept tight personal control over the sect's beliefs, writing all the doctrinal expositions themselves, Knorr was content to be the chief executive in an increasingly bureaucratic organisation. Because he was willing to share power, the Society, rather than the leader, became all important. This trend continued when Knorr's vice-president, F.W. Franz, succeeded to the leadership in 1977. The Watch Tower Bible and Tract Society provides probably the most tightly-knit bureaucratic organisation of any sect in the world today.

In this respect, it is important to be aware of the hierarchical structure which controls the movement. At the top there is a powerful triumvirate of the president, the vice-president, and the secretary-treasurer. Of almost equal authority, are another fourteen members (four of whom are fellow-directors of the first three) who, with the triumvirate, make up the sect's governing body. This governing body is identified with 'the faithful and wise servant' of Matthew 24.45 and is claimed to be the body to whom Jehovah has given the sole authority of interpreting the scriptures. It makes all the important decisions and formulate the sect's policy on every issue that arises.

The 211 countries in which Jehovah's Witnesses work are arranged in branches. The branch committee of each is directly responsible to the sect's governing body for the territory covered by the branch. Regular inspection of the branch's work is undertaken by zone overseers, and occasionally by higher officials. More locally, there are three levels in the structure. A number of congregations form a circuit and several circuits make up a district. District overseers, circuit overseers, and congregation elders form links between the sect's governing body and the local congregation.

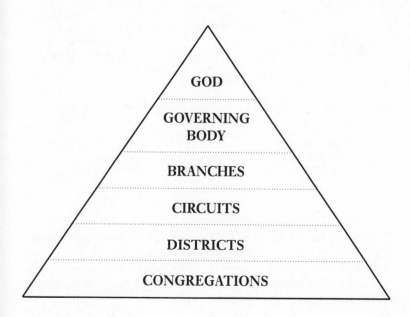

The Society has built up procedures which are designed to ensure that no one is able to build up a personal following by virtue of his office. They apply to all officials at every level. In an average congregation of about a hundred members, for example, each of five elders changes office on 1st January each year, moving in a strict sequence of theocratic school overseer, Watchtower overseer, Bible study overseer, field service overseer, and presiding overseer. At circuit and district level, overseers move on to other posts of responsibility after two years. At branch level, the committee, which may have from three to seven members depending on the size of the branch, also applies the rotation principle to its chairmanship, a branch chairman being expected to vacate his office in favour of his successor on 1st January each year.

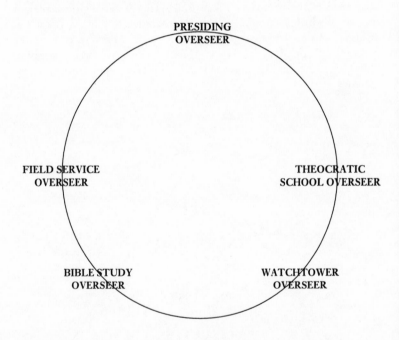

So firmly has the danger of a personality-cult been stamped out, that the movement's books no longer bear the names of their authors but are published anonymously. Moreover, official letters to those outside the movement often bear no personal signature but are simply stamped with the Society's name.

Although this may be disconcerting for non-members, to members it presents no problems. Jehovah's Witnesses believe what the Society tells them to believe, behave in the way the Society instructs them to behave, and do what the Society orders them to do. As far as they are concerned, the Society's governing body is the only legitimate and trustworthy interpreter of God's Word, the Bible. The governing body speaks for God. That is the most significant fact that mainstream Christians have to face if they wish to try to understand Jehovah's Witnesses.

JEHOVAH'S WITNESS MOTIVATION

Throughout their history, Jehovah's Witnesses have blazed the trail in religious outreach. The zeal with which they work has been the envy, and often the admiration, of many mainstream Christian churches. Why do they work so hard? There are at least four reasons.

1. They believe they have a God-given message for the whole world. As we shall see, this is a very different message from that of the Christian churches which, they believe, have distorted God's truth, teach error, and are therefore working for Satan.

2. They believe that the Battle of Armageddon is just round the corner. With the end of the world imminent, people must be persuaded to become Jehovah's Witnesses, for therein lies their only hope of survival.

3. They appear to believe that their own salvation depends on this door-to-door activity. By doing it, they demonstrate their obedience, their loyalty to Jehovah.

4. The Society expects them to do it. When all else fails, this is probably what still motivates them. Targets are set, areas allotted, and reports are expected by the Society – And for all practical purposes the Society means God.

JEHOVAH'S WITNESS STRATEGY

The overall aim of the movement's missionary strategy is to make contact with every member of the population and to persuade as many of them as possible to become Jehovah's Witnesses. The movement is totally mobilised to achieve this. No one is exempt, from the sect's president to its rawest recruit.

Ordinary members, who do full-time secular jobs and have to fit their religious activities into their spare time, are expected to give ten hours a month to this 'service work', as it is called. 'Pioneers', Witnesses who do only part-time secular jobs, may give a hundred hours a month. 'Special pioneers', full-time Jehovah's Witness workers, spend 140 hours visiting on behalf of the movement.

They must then submit to their local leaders records of visits made and results obtained. They run the risk of a stern admonition if they fail to achieve their set targets. So in almost every town and village, all the year round, but especially on Saturdays and Sundays, Jehovah's Witnesses of all ages can be seen busily working from door to door. The purpose of most of the local congregation's activity at the Kingdom Hall is to train and equip members for this work.

Although their tactics may vary slightly from place to place, Witnesses keep to a fairly stereotyped and well-tried pattern.

SEVEN STEPS TO COMMITMENT

1 Initial contact

2 Back call

3 Home study group

4 Congregational book studies

5 Kingdom Hall

6 Door-to-door visiting

7 Baptism

Step One – Initial Contact

Most readers will be familiar with this initial contact, for almost everyone living in Britain has been approached by a Jehovah's Witness at some time. Two Witnesses come to the door (or sometimes confront the contact on the street corner). They introduce themselves as those who would like to talk about God, or the Bible, or morality, or some recent disaster or current problem. At first they may not disclose the fact that they are Jehovah's Witnesses. Much of what they say at this stage may not seem to be very controversial. Their first aim is to win a hearing and to leave a piece of the movement's literature with the contact.

Step Two – Back Call

If the contact shows interest in their message and agrees to take their literature, he will be named in their records as an interested person worthy of a follow-up visit. This point needs to be underlined. Many people make the mistake of thinking that by taking a magazine (*Watchtower* or *Awake*) or some other book they will get rid of Jehovah's Witnesses. One of the best ways of ensuring further visits is to accept literature. The contact is then marked down in their records for a back-call. During this second visit the Witnesses will be concerned, not merely to discuss religion and to find out what the contact thought of the literature, but also to persuade the contact to receive further instruction.

Step Three – Home Study Group

The Jehovah's Witnesses will now want to urge the contact to allow them or some colleagues to come to his home to lead an informal Bible study for him and his family or friends. 'Let's forget about the churches and simply study together what God has to say in his Word', will be a typical approach at this stage. In reality the purpose of such sessions is to familiarise the contact with one of the sect's latest books. Although the Bible is used, texts are taken out of their context in an attempt to show their support for the movement's views. There will be no scope for differences of interpretation. The 'true' and only acceptable view will be the official line being laid down in the book being studied.

Step Four – Congregational Book Studies

If the contact's interest persists, the next step will be to persuade that person to join a larger group meeting in the area. This will consist of some fellow 'enquirers', like himself, and some committed Jehovah's Witnesses. Here the pattern of study will be as before, a study of one of the sect's books. The overriding aim will be to condition the contact to think as a Jehovah's Witness thinks. Only then will he or she be ready for the next stage.

Step Five – Kingdom Hall

The Kingdom Hall is the meeting place of the local Jehovah's Witness congregation. Depending upon the density of Witnesses in a particular area, it may serve two or three different congregations who arrange their programmes so that they can meet at different times. There are now about 75,000 of these congregations world-wide and 1,388 of them in Britain. Jehovah's Witnesses do not usually invite 'outsiders' to their Kingdom Hall meetings straight away but wait until the potential converts have been prepared by weeks of 'pre-evangelism'. Then when they arrive at the Kingdom Hall, people are given a warm welcome and every effort is made to integrate them into the congregation. Those whose interest still persists begin attending regularly. Every Sunday they will meet to study the latest edition of *The Watchtower* and will be expected to attend weekday classes to learn more of the sect's doctrines and training sessions to equip them to communicate those doctrines to others.

Step Six – Service Work

When it is obvious that interest is more than casual, the contact will be introduced to 'service work', the Witnesses name for door-to-door visiting. A pair of Witnesses working from door-to-door is likely to be an established Witness and a novice. The task of the established Witness is to train the novice. As stated earlier, the movement does not recognise people as members (or publishers as the call them) unless they are engaged in door-to-door work, but some 40 per cent of the movement's nominal membership (indicated by the number attending the annual Memorial) are engaged in this activity.

Step Seven – Baptism

People actively involved in service work and who now wish to commit themselves totally as Jehovah's Witnesses, are baptised by immersion as a sign of dedication to Jehovah. Such baptisms usually take place in a swimming pool during one of the movement's area conventions.

JEHOVAH'S WITNESS TRAINING

Ministerial Training

One of the most significant actions of Knorr's presidency came in 1942 when he started the Watch Tower Bible School of Gilead in New York State. This has been described by the movement's official history as 'a ministerial school of advanced training to equip missionaries and ministerial representatives for specialised service in foreign fields'.[4] It is claimed that 'the sending out of Gilead graduates has resulted in the building up of the organisation ... in many lands as well as the opening up of many new lands in which to establish congregations and branches of the Watch Tower Society'.[5] Clearly Gilead has been a kind of staff college, equipping the senior levels of the sect's leadership for their work.

More recently a new Ministerial Training School was established at Coraopolis in Pennsylvania. Its purpose is 'to equip men with spiritual qualifications to take on further organisational responsibilities'.[6] After completing an intensive eight-week course, which includes Bible study, administration, public speaking, and some attention to the participants' spiritual development, graduates are sent to work in various countries where the movement is active. The importance of this new development can be seen in the fact that three members of the Watch Tower Society's governing body helped staff the inaugural course.

Congregational Worship

Throughout almost the whole of Rutherford's presidency, worship (as commonly understood in the mainstream churches) was given a very low profile. One of the early casualties was hymn singing, but this was reintroduced by Knorr in 1944 along with the publication of The Kingdom Service Song Book. Prayer in the congregation is always extempore. There is an annual Memorial, the sect's version of the communion service of mainstream Christian churches. Only a handful of Witnesses actually partake of the bread and the wine, though all members attend. The numbers attending are considered important enough to warrant a mention in the movement's Yearbook: 12,288,917 attended in April 1994. Jehovah's Witnesses still stress that their worship is functional, not formal. By this they mean that they concentrate on equipping members for the spreading of the movement's teachings rather than on the kind of worship characteristic of most mainstream Christian churches.

Witnesses are expected to take part in the following meetings.

The Watchtower Study

This takes the place of the main act of worship found in mainstream Christian churches. The hour-long study is devoted to the latest edition of *The Watchtower*, which members will be expected to have studied individually before coming to the meeting. The method of study is identical in all congregations throughout the world. Directed by *The Watchtower* overseer, members follow the magazine's study article in their own copies as it is read aloud by one of their number. The overseer then draws attention to the questions at the foot of each page and encourages members to answer these aloud in an orderly manner, putting up their hands and waiting to be invited to answer. Children, as well as adults, are expected to participate. The acceptable answers are those which take the form of a resume of the answers given already in the printed text, though participants are encouraged to re-phrase these in their own words. The object of the exercise is that members should demonstrate in their answers that they have grasped the article's teaching.

The Public Talk

An hour-long lecture, based on an outline provided by the Society and delivered by one of its accredited speakers, precedes *The Watchtower* Study. Though intended primarily for non-Witnesses living nearby, members are also expected to attend. This means that on Sundays most Witnesses are committed to at least a two-hour session of intensive study in addition to any door-to-door work they do that day.

The two main weeknight meetings are the Service Meeting and the Theocratic Ministry School. These are usually held on the same evening and become, in effect, another two-and-a-half hour training session.

The Service Meeting

The aim of this meeting is to equip members 'to have an effective share in carrying out the work of preaching the Kingdom good news and making disciples'.[7] In the course of a year its carefully structured programme will outline scriptural methods of field work, effective methods of witnessing, and answers to objections, will train members to conduct home Bible studies, and will encourage them to share successful experiences in outreach.

The Theocratic Ministry School

This is an educational course for men, women and children within the congregation. The curriculum laid down by the Society includes courses on public speaking, conducting meetings, preaching, publicity techniques, and tactics in door-to-door work. This is one of the most important elements of Jehovah's Witness training and accounts very largely for the confidence displayed by Witnesses in their attempts to communicate their views to others.

Congregational Book Studies

These studies normally take place in the homes of members. Groups of up to twenty meet under the direction of a Book Study Overseer to study one of the Watch Tower handbooks. The study method will be that used in the Sunday study of *The Watchtower*. Up to ten different groups will be associated with any one congregation. All members are expected to participate. The group's overseer is responsible, not only for leading the book study, but also for leading the door-to-door work of the members of his group and for their pastoral care.

Total Commitment

In addition to all these meetings, Jehovah's Witnesses are expected to fulfil their monthly quota of door-to-door visits and, where necessary, to follow these up with study sessions in contacts' homes. Because of all these activities, zealous Witnesses have little time to pursue private interests. Former Witnesses have often remarked on the sense of complete emptiness they felt when first breaking away from the sect and the difficulties they experienced in trying to form satisfactory relationships with other people, for as Witnesses they found little time for friendships outside the movement.

WHAT JEHOVAH'S WITNESSES BELIEVE

Authority

Jehovah's Witnesses claim that their beliefs are derived directly from the Bible, which, they say, they accept as the authoritative Word of God. A Watch Tower publication says, 'The Bible is the truth, God's Word. If we follow it faithfully we shall not be misled ... The holy Bible can be proved to be the one sacred book of divine truth'.[8] One of their chief criticisms of mainstream Christianity is that the churches have all departed from the plain teachings of the Bible, replacing these with their own man-made and devil-inspired religious dogma.

Despite their claim to be a Bible-only group, however, the truth is that in practice they are a Bible-plus group. They do not claim additional revelation (as the Mormons do), but they do claim that their organisation alone can produce the only true and legitimate interpretations of the biblical material. This means that Witnesses are never encouraged to read the Bible with an open mind and to draw their own conclusions. They are expected to accept without question what Watch Tower publications tell them to believe. There is no room for disagreement even on the smallest points.

As noted earlier, the sect's justification for this attitude is based on an unusual interpretation of Matthew 24.45, 'Who is the trusty servant, the sensible man charged by his master to manage his household staff and issue their rations at the proper time?'. The Watch Tower view is that the 'trusty servant', or, to use their own jargon, 'the discreet slave class', consists of a small but elite group of Witnesses from whom the rest of Jehovah's Witnesses obtain their spiritual food. The spiritual food is the one and only correct interpretation of the Bible. This means that whatever is passed down from the sect's Brooklyn headquarters, generally by way of *The Watchtower*, is regarded as Jehovah's truth.

Interpretations of biblical passages passed down to members in this way illustrate how adept this 'discreet slave class' is at using the Bible to prove its own points. Watch Tower dogmas are read back into texts, usually without reference to their biblical context. An interesting example of this technique is the way the group's leaders use passages like Leviticus 3.17, 7.26f, and 17.10-14 to try to find a biblical basis for their objections to blood transfusions. Arguing from such passages, they assert that those willingly allowing themselves or their dependants to receive blood by transfusion run the risk of forfeiting eternal life for themselves and them. Over the years many Witnesses have died from relatively simple road accident injuries, because they refused transfusions which would have saved their lives. Studied in context, the Leviticus passages have nothing to say about blood transfusions but set out the Mosaic law banning the drinking of animal blood.

Jesus Christ

Arguing from the New Testament evidence, orthodox Christians believe that Jesus Christ is both God and man. The first disciples knew Jesus as a real human being, living and working among them. As time passed, however, and their experience of him deepened, they were compelled to acknowledge that, although he was truly human, he was not merely human. His life, his claims, his miracles, and finally the vindication of his resurrection, led them to recognise that in dealing with him they were dealing with God. Thomas was speaking for them all when he confessed, 'My Lord and my God',[9] and Jesus accepted that as a true estimate of his person. It is not surprising to find, therefore, that the writer of the Fourth Gospel has no doubts about Christ's deity. His opening words state, 'When all things began, the Word already was. The Word dwelt with God, and what God was, the Word was.'

Jehovah's Witnesses deny Christ's essential deity. Though prepared to speak of him as divine, they refuse to acknowledge him as God in the full sense of that word. They maintain that whereas Christ is 'a god', the Father, Jehovah, is 'the God'. So for them Christ is a secondary or demi-god. To maintain this view, Jehovah's Witnesses have re-translated John 1.1 to read, 'Originally the Word was, and the Word was with God, and the Word was a god' (The New World Translation). They claim that the original language of the New Testament supports this view. In reality, the Greek text does nothing of the kind. It means what Christians have always believed it to mean, that Christ was fully God – 'What God was, the Word was'.

Because Christians believe in the deity of Christ, they also recognise his eternity. Christ is God, and God is eternal: therefore Christ is eternal. The Son has always existed as the eternal Son of God. Jehovah's Witnesses reject this view. They are ready to admit that Christ had an existence prior to his birth in Bethlehem, but because they recognise only the Father (or Jehovah as they prefer to call him) as fully God, they do not believe that Christ has existed eternally. So they believe in Christ's pre-existence but deny his eternity, maintaining that there was a time when Jehovah-God was all alone in universal space and that when Jehovah began to create, his first creative act was his Son.

They claim to find biblical evidence for this belief mainly in two verses, Colossians 1.15, where Christ is described as 'the firstborn of all creation', and Revelation 3.14, where he is called 'the beginning of God's creation'. Other interpretations of these verses do not support the Jehovah's Witness view. In Colossians 1.15 the Greek for 'firstborn' is *prototokos*, which can mean 'the first' and 'the chief' as well as 'the firstborn', but does not mean 'the first-created', as Jehovah's Witnesses allege. The context shows that the main point at issue is Christ's superiority over creation, not his relationship to the Father. The mainstream Christian interpretation is that Paul means Christ is supreme over creation and heir of all things.

Turning to Revelation 3.14, everything depends on what is meant by 'the beginning'. Christians believe it means that Christ is the one through whom God's creative work was done. Christ is 'the beginning of God's creation' because he began it. That 'the beginning' need not be interpreted in the Jehovah's Witness way is indicated clearly in Revelation 21.6, where God himself is described as 'the beginning and the ending'. Not even Jehovah's Witnesses claim that God was the first one to be created and that he has an end!

Christians believe, therefore, that Colossians 1.15 and Revelation 3.14 support the orthodox view of Christ's eternity, rather than the Jehovah's Witness view of Christ's creatureliness. The New English Bible renders the two verses, 'his is the primacy over all created things' and he is 'the prime source of all God's creation'. The Good News Bible is even more explicit: 'Christ is ... superior to all created things' and is 'the origin of all that God has created'. Christians believe that by a miraculous act of God the child born to Mary was both God and man.[10] He was not only God, nor was he merely man; he was and is a unique Person, God and man. So, on the one hand, the writer to the Hebrews could say that Jesus 'in every respect has been tempted as we are'[11] because of his humanity, and, on the other hand, Thomas could confess, 'My Lord and my God'[12] because of Christ's deity.

Jehovah's Witnesses repudiate this idea of incarnation, maintaining instead that the life-force of the pre-existent Son was transferred from heaven to the womb of the virgin Mary. The result was that Jesus was born as a man, no more and no less. They often misunderstand the Christian view, mis-state it and then ridicule a view of Christ that mainstream Christians do not hold. Russell, for example, claimed that Christians believed that Jesus assumed a human body by a kind of materialisation such as that of the angels who appeared to Abraham in Genesis 18. Rutherford maintained that incarnation involved the belief that Jesus was a spirit-being and that his flesh was merely a covering or house in which this spirit-being lived. A more recent Watch Tower book repeats this as 'a spirit person clothed with flesh'.[13] It must be stated that these views are not a fair representation of the Christian doctrine of incarnation. Jehovah's Witnesses of course have every right to disagree with the Christian view if they so desire, but they should not misrepresent the Christian view and then condemn Christians for views which no orthodox Christian holds.

The Work of Christ

Turning from who Christ is to what he was sent to do, we find that the Cross is central to all that the New Testament says on this subject. Christians are shown that they cannot earn their salvation. They, together with the rest of the human race, are sinners whom Christ died to save. Because Christ died and thus paid sin's penalty, all may be forgiven and restored to fellowship with God. Christians therefore rejoice in the New Testament assurance that, when a person puts his trust in Christ, his sins are forgiven, he is reconciled to God, he is born again, and he receives God's gift of eternal life.

Jehovah's Witnesses deny these New Testament truths. Instead, they hold that by his death Christ has simply redeemed us from physical death and that, as we trust him and work for Jehovah now, we are assured of partaking in the resurrection hereafter. That resurrection will be to what Jehovah's Witnesses call life under favourable conditions, where there will be a fair test of loyalty to Jehovah. Those who successfully pass through this second probationary period will be rewarded with ever-lasting life – for the few in heaven but for the majority on earth. Everyone else will be annihilated. Clearly, the Watch Tower way of salvation is a 'do-it-yourself' enterprise, for in their scheme salvation depends upon what we do rather than upon what Christ has done.

In contrast mainstream Christians believe that Christ has redeemed us, not merely from physical death, but from the guilt and power of sin.[14] Those who put their trust and confidence in Christ are assured of eternal life here and now.[15] They are not (as the Jehovah's Witnesses teach) called to work for eternal life under 'favourable conditions' after they have died and been raised, but are invited to accept it as God's free gift here and now. So the New Testament states , 'God gave us eternal life, and this life is in his Son. He who has the Son has life; he who has not the Son of God has not life'.[16] The New Testament sweeps aside all human pretensions and every idea that we can earn God's favour. 'It is by his grace that we are saved, through trusting him; it is not your own doing. It is God's gift, not a reward for work done'.[17]

A Three-phased Christ

Jehovah's Witnesses divide Christ's existence into what amounts to three unconnected chronological phases.[18] As a pre-existent spirit being, he lived with Jehovah as the Archangel Michael. After his virgin birth, he existed on earth as a mere human being, no more and no less. At his resurrection, he was exalted as a divine spirit once more and ascended to his Father's right hand in invisible form. The sect's leaders have never tried to work out the theological implications of this view of a three-phase Christ. The least damaging thing that can be said about it is that there appears to be no real connection between the three phases. At worst, this view of Christ is moving towards three distinct beings, the pre-existent angelic Christ, the earthly human Jesus, and the risen and glorified Lord. On the basis of this strange Christology, however, Jehovah's Witnesses feel able to deny the bodily resurrection of Jesus, claiming that God miraculously removed and hid the dead body of the human Jesus. They then explain that the resurrected Christ materialised bodies when it suited his purpose to do this. The appearances are explained as temporary expediencies to support the first disciples, whose faith was not yet strong enough to accept the real truth of the risen spiritual Christ.

The Second Coming

The Witnesses go on to assert that this invisible Christ ascended to his exalted place at Jehovah's right hand until 1918, when, still as an invisible spirit, he returned to earth. Hence, Jehovah's Witnesses do not look for a future Second Coming of Christ, believing that it has already occurred as a culmination of the earth shaking events connected with the First World War.

Mainstream Christians believe the New Testament story is very different. The risen Christ had a real, though transformed, body.[19] When he ascended to his Father's side, humanity was exalted with and in him; and he now stands in the presence of God on our behalf.[20] One day he will return in majesty and glory and every eye will see him.[21]

The Holy Spirit

Jehovah's Witnesses regard the Spirit as an impersonal force, one of their doctrinal handbooks describing the Spirit as 'Jehovah's invisible energising force (greater than atomic energy) that produces visible results in many manifestations experienced by men'.[22] Another book, concluding a section which has attempted to show that the doctrine of the Trinity has no biblical foundation, asserts, 'As for the holy spirit with which Jesus was anointed, this spirit is not a person at all but is God's invisible active force by means of which God carries out his holy will and work'.[23] To the Witnesses, the Spirit is always 'it' and the name is never written in capital letters. They do not believe that every true servant of God has been born again of the Spirit,[24] but, as we shall see later, they limit the number of the born again to an elite body of 144,000.

In contrast, Christians believe that the Spirit is not merely an influence or an invisible force but a divine Person. Accepting New Testament teaching that the Spirit is one who teaches, bears witness, convicts, guides, and can be grieved, they maintain that these are characteristics of a person.[25] Moreover, to lie to the Spirit is to lie to God.[26] They believe that by the work of the Spirit within them they have been regenerated[27] and that the fruit of the Spirit is being produced in their lives.[28]

The Trinity

It will now be obvious that Jehovah's Witnesses completely reject the Christian doctrine of the Trinity. They believe it to be unscriptural and satanic. As we have seen, they believe that the one God, Jehovah, created a Son, Jesus Christ, and that this Son is god in a limited sense, god with a small 'g'. Moreover, they assert that Christians are wrong in describing 'holy spirit' as either God or Person, for to them 'holy spirit' is nothing more than God's invisible active force in the world.

The grounds on which Jehovah's Witnesses reject the Christian view are very similar to those which led Arius to reject it in the fourth century AD It is not surprising to find, therefore, that whereas the Christian Church pronounced Arius as a heretic and, more positively, set out the commonly accepted view of Christ in what we now know as the Nicene Creed, Jehovah's Witnesses applaud Arius as the champion of what they describe as the minority truth view.

The Elite

Jehovah's Witnesses believe in two grades of salvation. A total number of 144,000 elite will be rewarded with everlasting life in heaven, but the remainder of the redeemed will have to be content with everlasting life on earth.

The 'little flock', the 144,000 of The Book of Revelation, will go to heaven. They alone are the 'twice-born', the spirit-begotten sons of God, who will reign with Christ in the heavenly kingdom. Only those who feel sure in their hearts that they are members of this elite body actually partake of the bread and wine during the annual Memorial ceremony. In 1991 only 8,850 partook out of the 10,650,158 who attended. The implication to many Jehovah's Witnesses is that the total of the elite 144,000 has almost been completed from among Witnesses who have already died and that only a relatively small number of places remain to be filled. Hence most members do not expect to go to heaven. They are among that vast crowd of 'other sheep', faithful Jehovah's Witnesses who look forward to everlasting life on earth.

Mainstream Christians do not believe that the Book of Revelation requires such an interpretation. Revelation makes great use of poetic imagery and uses numbers symbolically. Moreover, the 144,000 mentioned in Revelation 7 are the 'sealed' out of 'every tribe of the sons of Israel'.[29] If this part of the chapter is taken literally, it refers to the number of *Jews* in heaven. Somewhat inconsistently, however, Jehovah's Witnesses interpret the number 144,000 literally and the 12,000 of each tribe symbolically.

Most commentators would interpret the whole passage symbolically. Some say it represents the saved under the old covenant. Others, understanding 'Israel' as the church, the true Israel of God, say it refers symbolically to the totality of the New Testament saints. However the 144,000 is interpreted, it is worth remembering that the passage mentions another great multitude 'which no man could number' who were 'standing before the throne and before the Lamb'.[30] The 'other sheep' of John 10.16 does not refer to believers who do not expect to go to heaven, but to those Gentiles who had yet to hear Christ's message. Moreover, far from recognising any distinction between these 'other sheep' and the 'sheep', or any two-graded everlasting life, Jesus promises that 'there shall be one flock, one shepherd'.

The Jehovah's Witnesses claim that the Body of Christ is 'limited to 144,000' lacks New Testament support. On the contrary, Paul addresses *all* the Roman Christians, *all* the Corinthians Christians, *all* the Ephesian Christians, and *all* the Colossian Christians as members of Christ's Body.[31] Similarly, the writer to the Hebrews appeals to all his readers to remember their fellow-Christians who are suffering on the grounds that they are all 'in the body'.[32] The teaching of the New Testament seems clear. Every Christian is a member of Christ's Body.

The Future

As we saw earlier, Jehovah's Witnesses do not expect a visible return of the exalted Christ, but claim that the second coming took place in 1918. They now await the end of the present world system which, they believe, will begin with the Battle of Armageddon. At that battle, they claim, all the religious and political systems of the world will be ranged against Jehovah and his faithful Witnesses. Every earthquake, famine, and large-scale catastrophe is seen as a sign that the end is imminent. Such disasters act as powerful incentives to the Witnesses in their proselytising activities, for Witnesses firmly believe that only those who align themselves with Jehovah by becoming members of their movement will survive Armageddon. The remainder of the human race will be annihilated.

After Armageddon, the devil will be locked up and there will be a thousand years of peace and life under 'favourable conditions'. During this millennium, Jehovah's Witnesses will be actively reproducing in order that the world may be repopulated. Everyone will live to the end of that thousand years, but then will come the last and final test. The devil will be released for a short time to test those who have been born during the millennium and have never been put to the test as to their loyalty to Jehovah. Those who survive this second probationary period will go on to live for ever, 144,000 of them in heaven but the vast majority here on earth.

WHERE WITNESSES AND MAINSTREAM CHRISTIANS PART COMPANY

JEHOVAH'S WITNESSES	CHRISTIANS
The Bible	
God's infallible Word but members must accept it only as interpreted by the movement's governing body, the Watch Tower Bible and Tract Society, who alone have the God-given right to decide what scripture means.	God has revealed all that he wants us to know of himself and his will for us in Christ, his incarnate Word and what we know of Christ is contained in the Bible, his written word. The Bible is the norm by which all claims to religious truth are to be measured, including those of religious leaders.
God	
God is one Person, Jehovah. All other beings have been created by him, including his Son. The traditional Christian idea of God as trinity is pagan in origin and is rejected.	God is Trinity, three divine Persons, Father, Son and Holy Spirit, within the unity of the Godhead.

JEHOVAH'S WITNESSES	CHRISTIANS

Christ

Jesus Christ, God's Son and God's Word, is not God in the full sense but a secondary or demi-god, god with a small 'g'. He was created by Jehovah and is inferior to him. He pre-existed as the archangel Michael before being born as a man. Whilst on earth he was not God incarnate but a human being, no more and no less.

Jesus Christ is God's eternal Word who became incarnate at his human birth. He did not then cease to be God but ceased to be treated as God. As God-made-man, he showed us what God is like and is the unique God-given Saviour for the human race.

The Holy Spirit

Holy Spirit is God's active but impersonal force at work in the world today. The Spirit is described as 'it' and is not the third person of the trinity, for the doctrine of the Trinity is rejected as pagan.

The Holy Spirit is the third Person of the Trinity, who not only works throughout God's universe to achieve God's purposes but also brings people to new life in Christ and dwells within and empowers each Christian believer.

Christ's death

Christ did not die on a cross but on a torture stake. His death does not guarantee eternal life for anyone. As a ransom for Adam's sin, it gives those who believe in Christ a second chance to earn eternal life under favourable conditions after they have been raised from death.

Christ's death on the cross is the ground of our salvation, for in Christ God was reconciling the world to himself. Achieved by the One who died and rose again for us, salvation is therefore not something we can earn but God's free gift received by grace and through faith.

JEHOVAH'S WITNESSES	CHRISTIANS

The People of God

Jehovah's Witnesses alone are Jehovah God's faithful servants and the only true Christians. Dedicated to Jehovah by baptism, they have identified themselves with him and placed themselves under his rule. All other people, whether or not they claim any religious affiliation, have aligned themselves with Satan, not God. This includes those who belong to the churches of Christendom, whose leaders are believed to be working for Satan.

The People of God, the Church, consists of all who through repentance and faith have accepted Jesus as Saviour and acknowledge him as Lord. Having identified themselves with Christ in his death and resurrection, symbolised and sealed by baptism, they are members of the Body of Christ and seek to serve God in his world. Despite their differences and denominations, they believe their essential unity is to be found in Christ, not in an earthly organisation.

The Second Coming

The Second Coming of Christ is past, having occurred invisibly in 1918. The Battle of Armageddon and the subsequent end of the present world, however, is imminent. Those who have joined Jehovah's Witnesses will survive Armageddon. Those who demonstrate their loyalty to Jehovah throughout the following millennium will be rewarded with everlasting life, for most on earth and for 144,00 in heaven.

The Second Coming is a sure and certain hope promised in the Bible. The whole of history will then reach its climax and the Kingdom of God will come in all its fullness . All the faithful, will then enjoy God's presence eternally, and will be transformed into the kind of people that God has always intended them to be.

See also comments on pages 84–85.

REFERENCES

1. *Jehovah's Witnesses in the Divine Purpose*, p.1.
2. ibid p.62
3. *Qualified to be Ministers*, p.315.
4. *Jehovah's Witnesses in the Divine Purpose*, p.202.
5. *Let Your Name Be Sanctified*, p.343.
6. *1992 Yearbook of Jehovah's Witnesses.*
7. *Your Word is a Lamp to My Foot*, p.52.
8. *Things in Which it is Impossible for God to Lie*, p.31.
9. John 20.28.
10. Luke 1.35; 2.11; Galatians 4.4; etc.
11. Hebrews 4.15.
12. John 20.28.
13. *Things in Which it is Impossible for God to Lie*, p.231.
14. Romans 3.23-28, Galatians 1.4, 3.13, 1 John 1.6-10, 3.5.
15. John 3.36, 5.24, Romans 6.23.
16. 1 John 5.11-12.
17. Ephesians 2.8-9.
18. J.F. Rutherford, *The Harp of God* (1928) p.103.
19. Luke 24.37-43.
20. Hebrews 9.24.
21. Acts 1.11; Revelation 1.7.
22. *Make Sure of All Things*, 1953, p.360.
23. *Things in Which it is Impossible for God to Lie* p.269.
24. John 3.5, etc.
25. John 14-16.
26. Acts 5.3f.
27. John 3.
28. Galatians 5.22-23.
29. Revelation 7.4.
30. Revelation 7.9.
31. Romans 12.4-5, 1 Corinthians 10.17, Ephesians 1.23, Colossians 3.15.
32. Hebrews 13.3.

Chapter 3
THE CHRISTADELPHIANS

Like most of the sects on the Christian perimeter, the Christadelphians originated in America during the nineteenth century. Unlike most others, however, this movement was founded by an Englishman.

HOW THEY ORIGINATED

John Thomas

Thomas, the son of a Congregational minister, was born in London on 12th April 1805. After studying medicine at St Thomas's Hospital, London, and qualifying as an MRCS, he sailed for America in 1832 intending to practise in that country. Having survived a shipwreck on the way, however, he felt he owed it to God to devote the rest of his life to religion.

At first, he aligned himself with Alexander Campbell, who in 1827 had founded a movement known as the Disciples of Christ. This movement, soon nicknamed the Campbellites, emphasised the importance of baptism by immersion, taught that the second coming of Christ was imminent, claimed to base its teaching entirely on the Bible, and rejected all the existing credal statements of mainstream Christianity. Thomas was baptised by the Campbellites and began to preach under their auspices. It was not long, however, before he became dissatisfied with the Campbellites, and in particular with their practice of baptising people before, in Thomas' view, they were prepared intellectually for this important step. So Thomas forsook the group and struck out on his own.

When he first landed in America, he had continued to practise medicine alongside his religious activities and was awarded an American MD in 1848. Eventually, however, he forsook medicine and began working fulltime to spread his religious views. He then founded the Christadelphians, whose name means 'brothers in Christ', a name that was intended to distinguish his followers from the many people who, in Thomas' view, unworthily described themselves as Christians.

A keen student of the Bible, Thomas became so convinced that his own interpretations of scripture were the only correct ones that he rejected many of the beliefs of orthodox Christianity. He came to believe that only those who accepted his views and became Christadelphians could be saved. In 1834 he began to publish his views in a magazine called *The Apostolic Advocate* and followed this in 1844 with *The Herald of the Future Age*.

He returned to England for two years in 1848, preaching all over the country and writing what was to become a Christadelphian classic, *Elpis Israel – An Exposition of the Kingdom of God*. At first this rather heavy-going book was not well received, but when Thomas made a brief return visit to England in 1862, he found many small groups of Thomasites, as they were first known, meeting in various parts of the country, with flourishing Christadelphian centres in Birmingham, Nottingham, Halifax, Aberdeen, and Edinburgh. At first, the movement had no official headquarters. Members used to meet for breaking of bread cere-monies in each others houses. Soon, however, Birmingham began to emerge as the most influential centre, other Christadelphians looking to it for guidance and a supply of lecturers. It was during this second visit that Thomas wrote *Eureka*, a 2,000 page commentary on the Book of Revelation in which he claimed to have solved problems of interpretation which had baffled biblical scholars for years. By 1865 the membership of the movement had increased to a just a thousand, most of them located in Great Britain. Growth was steady if unspectacular, and three years later there were twenty-five Christadelphian assemblies (or 'ecclesias', as they were called) in England, four in Wales, and twelve in Scotland.

Robert Roberts

One of Thomas's earliest converts was Robert Roberts, who soon secured his position as leader of the movement in Britain by publishing a maga-zine called *The Ambassador of the Coming Age*. When Thomas made his third and final visit to England in 1869, he suggested that the magazine should be renamed *The Christadelphian*. Roberts succeeded as leader of the movement when Thomas died in 1871. From then onwards official Christadelphian views were disseminated through *The Christadelphian*. Birmingham has remained an influential centre for the main body of Christadelphians, though some splinter groups look elsewhere for their doctrinal leads.

Developing many of Thomas's embryonic ideas, Roberts gave a detailed treatment of his views in *Christendom Astray*. As its title suggests, this book sought to demonstrate the gulf between what Roberts saw as biblical Christianity and the generally accepted views of the mainstream

Christian churches. *Christendom Astray* has been reprinted many times and is still a standard Christadelphian textbook. In it Roberts argued that whereas the churches had turned their backs on the Bible, Christadelphianism was entirely Bible-based. Like Jehovah's Witnesses with whom they share some beliefs, therefore, Christadelphians claim to be a Bible-only group. By the time of Roberts' death in 1898, the Birmingham fellowship had become the standard of orthodoxy throughout Christadelphianism and *The Christadelphian* had been recognised as the movement's official mouthpiece.

CONTEMPORARY CHRISTADELPHIANISM

The Christadelphians have never attracted as much support as Jehovah's Witnesses, despite their similarities. This may be partly because they have never built up anything like the strong bureaucratic organisation headed by authoritarian leadership or developed an aggressive kind of outreach programme, both of which are so characteristic of Jehovah's Witnesses. Consequently, the movement has never been widespread, and although Christadelphians have been fairly well established in Britain for a century and a half their membership has never been high. Today there are probably about 20,000 British Christadelphians in a little over 300 congregations, and about another 20,000 in the rest of the world.

Christadelphianism is essentially a lay movement: there are no professional clergy or ministers. Local ecclesias are run by male members. A high proportion of the movement's membership takes a full part in its activities. Regular meetings include a weekly breaking-of-bread ceremony, a Sunday evening lecture intended for the public at large but supported mainly by members, a weekly Bible class, and a women's meeting. Evangelistic outreach is done through public lectures, personal contacts, well-organised and well-publicised Bible exhibitions, and literature.

Although the official stance of the movement is that the Christian churches have largely departed from the teachings of the Bible, Christadelphians are often prepared to join with mainstream Christians for Bible study and other activities. Where they find it necessary to disagree with others, they usually do so politely and with dignity.

WHAT CHRISTADELPHIANS BELIEVE
The Bible

Like their founder, Christadelphians recognise the supreme authority of the Bible, which they prefer in the Authorised Version of 1611. As well as

attending a weekly Bible class, members follow a carefully planned course
of daily Bible readings. Like mainstream Christians, they claim to base
their beliefs and practices on the teachings of the scriptures.
Nevertheless, following the lead given at first by Thomas and subsequently by Roberts, they have consistently interpreted the Bible in ways
that differ significantly from the commonly held Christian views. In
particular, they reject a number of the basic doctrines held by mainstream
Christians and set out in the historic Christian creeds.

God

Like most sects on the Christian perimeter, Christadelphians deny the
mainstream Christian view of God as Trinity. Mainstream Christians
believe that the only view of God which does justice to the biblical
evidence is that which, whilst acknowledging that there is one God,
nevertheless recognises that within the Godhead the three Persons of
Father, Son, and Holy Spirit are coequal and coeternal.

The basis of the Christadelphian rejection of that view lies in the
teachings of their founder and his successor. Thomas's view was set out
in some detail in his classic, *Elpis Israel*, and more speculatively in
Phanerosis, a book which has proved something of an embarrassment to
some modern Christadelphians. In brief, Thomas stated that there is
only one Being, the Eternal God, whose deity is underived and who is
originally immortal in every sense. Below him, however, are a whole
host of elohim (the Hebrew word for God or gods), who were created by
him before the world was made and who were tested by him in some
other place. As a result of this successful probationary period, during
which they existed as mortal men, these elohim have now been raised to
the status of immortal and incorruptible beings. They are, in effect,
secondary gods. Similarly, it is possible for today's humans to become
tomorrow's elohim. Jesus has already blazed this trail, for though once a
man he has was raised to the nature of the elohim, the gods.

Roberts' teaching about God was much more cautious. Though he
followed some of Thomas's ideas, his main concern was, not to
speculate about the elohim, but to attack the Christian doctrine of the
Trinity. He asserted, 'Trinitarianism propounds – not a mystery, but a
contradiction – a stultification – an impossibility'.[1] How, he asked, could
God be called 'Father' unless he preceded and brought into existence
the Son? Developing another of Thomas's themes, Roberts tried to
discredit the Christian view that God, being Spirit, is without body or
parts, for he himself believed that God has a physical body with all its

organs. So, 'the Father is a tangible person'.[2] It is interesting to note the similarities between such views and those of the Mormons, set out on pages 28–30.

Present-day Christadelphians are as opposed to the doctrine of the Trinity as were Thomas and Roberts. The doctrine is regarded as a 'gross perversion' propounded by 'professors of Christianity' who allowed 'pagan speculation and their own imaginations to take over from the inspired teaching which the apostles of Jesus himself had been at such pains to furnish'. Nowhere in the Bible, Christadelphians argue, do we find the word 'trinity', 'nor do we find God presented in the pages of Scripture in the manner of the later "creeds" of Christendom, such as the Athanasian'.[3]

They appear to be divided, however, in their attitude to the earlier Christadelphian views about the elohim as 'secondary gods'. On the one hand, a previous editor of *The Christadelphian* told me, 'Generally Dr Thomas's teaching on the Elohim in Elpis Israel is accepted'.[4] He then qualified this by adding that an adequate summary of the Christadelphian view is that 'there is one Eternal God, the supreme, and there are beings of angelic rank who possess immortality, but as to how and when they attained that immortality the Scriptures are silent'. On the other hand, another Christadelphian writer denies Thomas's speculations, affirming, 'He is not the Supreme God among many Gods but the only God'.[5] That writer also told me, 'So far as I am able to follow Dr. Thomas's arguments, I cannot say that I find them altogether convincing ... and I am not alone in this'.[6]

That there are such differences of emphasis among modern Christadelphians is itself very interesting. Both Jehovah's Witnesses and Mormons would not display, or indeed countenance, such differences. The Watch Tower's governing body and the Mormon presidency are regarded as God's direct spokesmen within their respective organisations. The Christadelphian claim to submit to the authority of the Bible seems to carry more weight. Christadelphians are still faced with the problem that has always faced mainstream Christians in this respect, however, for people who unite in affirming the authority of scripture do not always agree about how the Bible is to be interpreted.

Jesus Christ

By rejecting the doctrine of the Trinity, Christadelphians deny three fundamental beliefs of orthodox Christians concerning the Person of Christ – his deity, his eternity, and his incarnation.

Denial of Christ's Deity

Because they believe that the Father alone is God in the full sense, Christadelphians deny Christ's deity. A Christadelphian publication asserts: 'The Bible teaches that Jesus Christ is not the very essence of the Godhead ... but is the only-begotten Son of God, born of the virgin Mary at a set time'.[7] Christadelphians are happy to describe Jesus (as does St Paul) as 'the express image' of God's Person. Nevertheless, they refuse to find in that description a justification for the mainstream Christian doctrine of Christ's deity. 'The word image conveys the idea of an exact likeness of the original. But to say that Jesus Christ was a perfect moral image of God as he walked among men is very different from saying, as the church creeds would say, that he was himself the very Godhead'.[8] Though ready to describe him as divine, therefore, Christadelphians regard his divinity as derived and therefore secondary. To them Christ occupies a position similar to that of the other elohim. In Thomas's terms he would seem to be one, perhaps the supreme one, of the numerous elohim created by God and who by their previous human lives of faith and obedience have earned the right to be raised to the divine status.

Denial of Christ's Eternity and Pre-existence

It follows that Christadelphians deny Christ's eternity and pre-existence. 'The Son only came into existence when the virgin Mary gave birth to Jesus'.[9] We have seen that Jehovah's Witnesses, following the ancient Arian heresy, claim that the Son of God was not eternal but came into existence at a distinct point in time. Nevertheless, Jehovah's Witnesses do recognise the Son's pre-existence, albeit as the archangel Michael. Christadelphians go much further than either Arians or Jehovah's Witnesses, maintaining that before the first Christmas day the Son had no prior existence at all, except as a thought in the mind of God.

Those familiar with the Bible will recall the great pre-existence passages of John's Gospel which require a very different viewpoint. Jesus says:

'I am that living bread which has come down from heaven' (6.51);

'God is the source of my being, and from him I come.
I have not come of my own accord; he sent me' (8.42);

'Before Abraham was born, I am' (8.58);

'I came from the Father and have come into the world.
Now I am leaving the world again and going to the Father' (16.28);

*'Father, glorify me in thine own presence with the glory
which I had with thee before the world began'* (17.5).

A number of other passages, including Philippians 2.5-11, Colossians
1.15-20, contain the same kind of teaching.

Some modern theologians escape the implications of such passages by
stating that the writer of the Fourth Gospel put these sayings into the
mouth of Jesus. This still leaves unanswered the question as to why he did
this. Presumably it was because this was what he and the first century
Church believed about Jesus, a point which is clearly confirmed by the
Philippian and Colossian passages. Is it too naive to suggest that they
themselves not only believed this about Jesus but believed it because that
was what Jesus had taught? Christadelphians shrink from such a critical
approach to the New Testament, claiming to take such scriptures at their
face value and believing them to be inspired and inerrant. So they have a
different explanation, believing that these and similar passages of scripture indicate no more than that the Son existed as a purpose in the divine
will. Orthodox Christians regard these passages at the very least as an
indication that Jesus, and a little later the Apostolic Church, were
conscious of his personal pre-existence with the Father.

Denial of the Incarnation

The Christadelphians then take a short but inevitable step from the denial
of Christ's deity, eternity and pre-existence to the rejection of his
incarnation. If he is not God in the full sense, and if he did not exist before
his human birth of the virgin Mary, then it cannot be affirmed that he
became man in the sense understood by mainstream Christians. In fact,
Christadelphians go on to assert that Jesus did not become the Christ
until he was baptised by John in the River Jordan. Thereafter, all through
his earthly life he remained man and it was not until he was raised from
the dead that his humanity was transformed into divinity. Jesus was then
'perfected', so that it can now truly be said that he is 'of the same nature
as God himself'.[11] This has to be understood against the background of
the Christadelphian doctrine of God, outlined earlier, for the 'nature'
which the Son now shares with the Father is derived. This comes close to
the Jehovah's Witness view that Jesus is god with a small 'g'. Denying the
orthodox Christian view that the risen Christ ascended to heaven as the
unique Lord, who is both God and man, therefore, Christadelphians
prefer to affirm that 'he is now the corporealization of life-spirit as it
exists in the Deity', whatever that means!

Readers familiar with the history of Christian doctrine will know that the kind of views of Christ's Person expressed by Christadelphians were well known almost from the beginning of the Christian Church. In *The Four Great Heresies*, J.W.C. Wand described how the author of John's Gospel found himself fighting on two fronts. On the one hand were those who were not convinced that Jesus was divine in the full sense, and on the other hand were those who were not convinced that he was really human. Whereas the first group tended to think of Jesus as a mere man, the others thought of him as a divine apparition. Wand went on to show how the two extremes persisted throughout the early history of the Church, resulting in the adoptionist heresies, on the one hand, and pneumatic heresies on the other.[12] Christadelphians are a modern version of adoptionists, for as we have seen they hold that Jesus is not God in the full sense but has been raised by God to some kind of divine status.

The Work of Christ

Christadelphians, like most mainstream Christians, interpret the work of Christ (what he came to do) as a fulfilment of the types prefigured in the Old Testament sacrificial system, which pointed to the need for a sacrifice to be made in order that sin might be taken away. The need for such sacrifice stems from the sin of Adam and Eve, whose disobedience of a direct divine command resulted in the sentence of physical death. Jesus died and rose for us. But how can Christ's achievement be of any help to us? The Old Testament sacrifices pointed the way. When a sinner offered a sacrifice to God he was acknowledging that sin merits death and can only be expiated by the shedding of blood. The Old Testament sacrifices 'impressed upon those who offered them the truth that sin can be atoned for only through the forfeiting of a life – and that a perfect life'. 'In this way the people of God were instructed in the principle of redemption through sacrifice, and the way was prepared for the coming of the perfect one'.[13]

'When the lifeless body of Jesus hung upon the cross, it was to outward appearances a triumph for sin, but in fact it was the conquest of sin. His life was willingly offered: it was a voluntary surrendering ... The moral perfection of Jesus' character rendered his sacrifice immeasurably superior to that of all the animals that ever were slain'.[14] 'It only remains for us to find out how we can be associated with Christ's sacrifice and the ensuing benefits'.[15]

How can we be identified with Christ in his death and resurrection? The Christadelphian answer is by baptism by immersion as an adult believer. Such baptism (unlike the sprinkling of infants) 'is a symbolic burial and resurrection. By submitting to this act, the believer acknowledges his past life to have been sin in the sight of God. He 'buries' it, and arises with a resolve to live a new kind of life – a Christ-like life as far as lies within his power'.[16] All of this is backed up by references to Romans 6. 'If we ally ourselves with Christ's sacrifice through baptism, God has promised to forgive our sins for Christ's sake'.[17] Therefore, 'Through the shed blood of Christ we have forgiveness. Moreover, this forgiveness is complete and it is everlasting ... so that even though we die, we need not fear death, for the God who raised Jesus on the third day will raise all his servants from death also'.[18] That being so, 'The cross of Christ is the focal point of God's plan for human redemption'.[19]

Leaving aside the particular questions that arise about the Christadelphians view of baptism, the rest sounds orthodox enough. How then does it tie up with other Christadelphians statements, such as the following?

'Nothing will save a man in the end but an exact knowledge of the will of God as contained in the Scriptures, and faithful carrying out the same', wrote Roberts.[20] Even allowing for some rhetorical over-emphasis in Roberts' statement, it indicates clearly the direction his thoughts were taking. Salvation resulted from a combination of an intellectual grasp of the Bible's teaching and a life of obedience.

Without wishing to go as far as Roberts, many mainstream Christians would wish to stress the importance of a rigorous application to the Christian faith of whatever intellect a person has been given. Moreover, no Christian who wished to take the claims of Christ seriously would wish to play down the importance of doing the will of God. 'If (faith) does not lead to action, it is in itself a lifeless thing.'[21] Nevertheless, mainstream Christians believe that obedient action is the result of God's grace in their hearts, not the ground of their salvation: we are not saved *by* good works but *for* good works. To go back to the kind of language Roberts used of the Spirit, the Christian life-style is a 'manifestation' of the work of God within us. Mainstream Christians would wish to distance themselves from Roberts' comment about salvation depending on 'an exact knowledge of the will of God', for imperfect human beings can never achieve such knowledge.

To this day, Christadelphians remain strongly opposed to the belief that we are justified through faith alone, considering it to be one of Christianity's corruptions. For them real faith does not appear to be the New Testament's trust in a person but mental assent to Christadelphian doctrines, and such faith is proved by a willingness to be baptized by immersion and the living of a good life. So they argue that infants and the insane cannot be saved, for both are incapable of indulging in this kind of intellectual exercise.

All of this is closely tied up with the Christadelphian belief that man has no inherent immortality. When animal man dies, Christadelphians believe, everything that there is of that person perishes. His hope for the future lies in resurrection. Therefore, those incapable of the required response (like infants and the insane) or who are unworthy (because of wickedness or a deliberate refusal to respond to God's Word) will not be raised.

It is hardly surprising to find, therefore, that Christadelphians have no assurance of salvation. After all, if my salvation depends upon what I do, rather than on what God in Christ has done for me, who may tell whether I have done enough to earn God's approval and to merit salvation? Even baptism, though regarded as indispensable to salvation, can do nothing more than make the Christadelphian 'a lawful candidate for that "birth of the spirit" from the grave, which will finally constitute him a "son of God, being of the children of the resurrection" ... His ultimate acceptance will depend upon the character he develops in this new relation'.[22]

Christadelphians believe that the cross was a declaration of God's righteousness. Roberts, explaining that view in *The Blood of Christ*, uses Romans 3.21-25 to back it. No student of the New Testament will wish to argue that this is not one aspect of the significance of the cross. For Roberts and his modern Christadelphian successors, however, it would appear to be the only aspect. They want nothing to do with the idea that Christ died instead of us, or that he paid the price of our sin.

The Kingdom

There is far more about the kingdom than about the cross in Christadelphian literature. The main emphasis of their Kingdom theology, however, is placed on prophecy. Briefly, their view is that God's promise to Abraham concerning the land of Canaan will be fulfilled literally at some future date. Then the Jews will be gathered in Palestine and the ancient Kingdom of Israel will be restored. Jesus will return to reign on earth. A new Temple will be erected and sacrifices will once more be offered. All the faithful will be raised to immortality, but the wicked will be annihilated. Closely linked with such teaching is their view that heaven is the abode of God alone. Human beings do not go there either at death or at any subsequent time.

The Holy Spirit

Christadelphians deny the personality but admit the eternity of the

Spirit. This is quite logical in their doctrinal system, for the Spirit is regarded as 'an unseen power emanating from the Deity, filling all space, and by which He is everywhere present ... It is the medium by which (God) upholds the whole creation'.[23] Christadelphians believe that it was this power that enabled the apostles to perform miracles and therefore deny that the Spirit dwells in believers today, otherwise, they say, believers would be able to perform similar miracles. So Roberts stated, 'There is no manifestation of the Spirit in these days. The power of continuing the manifestation doubtless died with the apostles'.[24]

This argument begs all kinds of questions. How do we define miracles? Are miracles the only manifestation of the Spirit's activity? In fact, since the development of the modern charismatic movement, there are many who would deny that the ages of miracles is over. There seems to be plenty of evidence of 'miraculous' healings to refute the Christadelphian claim. And are not lives transformed by Christ miracles of a different kind? Moreover, does not Galatians 5.22-25 suggest that some of the other manifestations of the Spirit are the harvest of love, joy, peace, patience, kindness, goodness, fidelity, gentleness, and self-control, seen in the lives of those in whom God is at work? Impervious to such arguments, however, the Christadelphian view remains unaltered. It has repercussions for the movement's doctrine of salvation, for Christadelphians do not believe that people are brought into a relationship with God through Christ as they respond to the work of the Holy Spirit within them.

WHERE CHRISTADELPHIANS AND MAINSTREAM CHRISTIANS PART COMPANY

CHRISTADELPHIANS	CHRISTIANS
The Bible	
The Bible, particularly in its 1611 Authorised Version, is regarded as the infallible Word of God, containing God's revelation of himself and of his requirements for his people. It is from the Bible that all Christadelphian beliefs and practices are said to be derived. On this basis, also, a number of mainstream Christian doctrines are rejected as being unscriptural.	God has revealed all that he wants us to know of himself and his will for us in Christ, his incarnate Word and what we know of Christ is contained in the Bible, his written word. The Bible is the norm by which all claims to religious truth are to be judged. The historic creeds and formularies of the Church are believed to represent faithfully the Bible's teaching.

CHRISTADELPHIANS	CHRISTIANS

God

The Eternal God is one being, who is tangible, and who alone inhabits heaven. He has raised the human Jesus to divine status following his resurrection. Some Christadelphians believe that other beings have also been raised to the status of gods (elohim) because of their worthiness and have become immortal and incorruptible. Other Christadelphians believe that the Supreme God is not one among others but the only God.	God is Trinity, three coequal and coeternal divine Persons, Father, Son , and Holy Spirit, within the unity of the Godhead.

Christ

Christadelphians have an adoptionist view of Christ. He is not the eternal Son of God and he had no pre-existence, except in the divine Mind, before his human birth. He became the Christ at his baptism. Following his death and resurrection, God raised him to divine status. Christ's incarnation is denied.	Jesus Christ is God's eternal Word who became incarnate at his human birth. He did not then cease to be God but ceased to be treated as God. As God-made-man, he showed us what God is like and is the unique God-given Saviour for the human race.

The Holy Spirit

The Spirit is an impersonal divine power through which God upholds the universe and through which the apostles were enabled to perform miracles. Today's believers are not filled with this power, otherwise they would be able to perform similar miracles to those of the apostles.	The Holy Spirit is the third Person of the Trinity, who not only works throughout God's universe to achieve God's purposes but also brings people to new life in Christ and dwells within and empowers each Christian believer.

CHRISTADELPHIANS	CHRISTIANS

Salvation

Christ's death on the Cross was the fulfilment of the Old Testament sacrificial system and demonstrated that the sacrifice of a perfect life had to be made to remove human sin. The cross was also a demonstration of God's righteousness. We benefit from what Christ did on the Cross as we identify ourselves with his death and resurrection through being baptised as adult believers, work at improving our knowledge of God through the scriptures, and obey him. The view that we are justified through faith alone is regarded as a corruption of the truth.	Christ's death on the cross is the ground of our salvation, for in Christ God was reconciling the world to himself. Achieved by the One who died and rose again for us, salvation is not something we earn by obedience or in any other way, but is God's gracious gift appropriated through trusting in Christ as Saviour, so salvation is by God's grace and through faith. Out of love for God and in thankful response to what he has done for us in Christ, we seek by his grace to live lives that accord with his will.

God's Kingdom

This is closely linked with prophetic teaching about the future. The Jews will be gathered in Palestine, the ancient kingdom of Israel will be restored, the temple rebuilt, sacrifices again offered, and Jesus will return to reign on earth. The faithful will become immortal and live on earth, but others will be annihilated. God alone will continue to inhabit heaven.	The Second Coming is a sure and certain hope promised in the Bible. The whole of history will then reach its climax and the Kingdom of God will come in all its fullness . All the faithful, will then enjoy God's presence eternally, and will be transformed into the kind of people that God has always intended them to be.

CHRISTADELPHIANS AND JEHOVAH'S WITNESSES

Several times in this chapter we have referred to some of the similarities between Christadelphians and Jehovah's Witnesses. Indeed, because of the close doctrinal similarities, the two are sometimes confused, to the annoyance of both Jehovah's Witnesses and Christadelphians! It may be helpful to summarise the main doctrinal similarities and differences.

- Both agree that only one Being and one Person is God in the full sense. All other divinity is therefore derived and secondary divinity.
- Both reject the mainstream Christian view that the eternal Son became incarnate and that Jesus is both God and man.
- Both deny the personality of the Holy Spirit, interpreting Spirit as God's power or influence.
- It follows that both are unequivocal in their denial of the Trinity. They regard it at best as a misinterpretation of scripture. At worst it is a modern version of Greek mythology or a complete fabrication inspired by Satan.

But there are some differences, particularly in their views of Christ.

Both agree that he has not existed from all eternity with the Father but came into existence at a distinct point in time. He is, therefore, a creature.

However:

- **Jehovah's Witnesses** believe the Son was God's first creative act. They accept the New Testament's teaching about the Son's pre-existence.
- **Christadelphians** believe the Son had no existence prior to his birth to the virgin Mary in Bethlehem. They reject the idea of his pre-existence and interpret all the New Testament pre-existence passages as pointing to the Son's 'existence' in God's thought, will, or intention.

Both movements follow the traditional view that Christ's atonement was made necessary by Adam's fall in the garden of Eden, but limit what was lost by Adam's fall to physical life. They each reject belief in the soul's immortality, regarding it as unscriptural and pagan. They also agree that the wicked will be annihilated. For both movements eternal life will mean a kind of physical life immortalised as a result of Christ's resurrection.

However:

- For **Jehovah's Witnesses** the meaning of the atonement revolves around the concept of 'ransom'. Christ as a perfect human being became the ransom to divine justice, restoring exactly what was lost through Adam's sin.

• For **Christadelphians** the meaning of the atonement revolves around the concept of 'kingdom', the cross being limited to a declaration of God's righteousness.

Moreover, their differences are not confined to doctrine. Both are concerned to spread their teaching, which they believe to be the sole legitimate interpretation of God's Word, the Bible.

However:

• **Jehovah's Witnesses** employ hard-sell tactics in their proselytising activities, which are used in a carefully planned strategy of outreach.

• **Christadelphians** are gentler, and much more staid, in their missionary activities. They rely largely on publicity and Bible exhibitions to win converts.

• In general, **Jehovah's Witnesses** are not prepared to discuss their differences, but state their views as the only option.

• Most **Christadelphians** are ready to talk quietly and reasonably about their faith and to listen to other people's points of view.

REFERENCES

1. Robert Roberts, *Christendon Astray*, page 77.
2. ibid page 79.
3. *Jesus Christ – God or Man?*, page 5.
4. John Carter's letter dated 21st November 1961.
5. E.J. Newman, *The God Whom We Worship*.
6. Letter dated 20th March 1962.
7. Jesus Christ – God or Man?, page 6.
8. ibid page 14.
9. J.J. Andrew, *The Real Christ*, page 71.
10. ibid page 74.
11. *The Four Great Heresies*, pages 23ff.
12. *The Cross of Christ*, page 11.
13. ibid.
14. ibid pages 13-14.
15. ibid.
16. ibid .
17. ibid.
18. ibid.
19. ibid.
20. ibid pages 57f.
21. James 2.17.
22. Roberts op. cit. pages 233-237.
23. J.J. Andrew op. cit. pp. 65f.
24. Roberts op. cit. page 86.

Chapter 4

THE FAMILY –
THE CHILDREN OF GOD

The Children of God, now generally known as The Family, emerged from the wider and more respectable 1960s Jesus Movement in the United States. Its members often appear as a group of evangelical Christians who have become disillusioned with traditional church life and have rejected that and the godlessness of western society. They have gained notoriety for their rejection of mainstream Christianity and traditional Christian moral values.

Their membership is very small – probably a few thousand worldwide, with about two hundred followers in Britain. Because of their persistent and sometimes aggressive outreach, their attempts to sell their literature, and the methods they have employed to raise money, the Children of God have stirred up controversy and attracted bad media coverage wherever they have gone.

DAVID BERG, alias MOSES DAVID

The Children of God, which originated in California some thirty years ago, were founded by David Berg, a former American Baptist minister. Berg's parents had been full-time evangelists of the American Christian and Missionary Alliance and he spent much of his early life travelling widely with them in their evangelistic work. He became pastor of a church in Arizona, but following a dispute with his congregation left them at the end of the Second World War. Moving to South California. Berg then became press officer for Fred Jordan, a Pentecostal minister involved in a radio ministry and pastoral counselling of young drop-outs.

A significant development occurred in 1968 when Berg settled in Huntingdon Beach and started 'Teens for Christ', a movement based on a communal pattern of living and intensive Bible study. Berg encouraged converts to leave their jobs and to drop out of society, which he taught them to regard as an evil system. Already he was beginning to display that strongly authoritarian style of leadership which is now a major characteristic of the Children of God. Members were expected to give him their unquestioning obedience.

Just over a year later Berg prophesied that God's judgement in the form of an earthquake was soon to fall on California. Teens for Christ came to an end, as Berg and those remaining loyal to him beat a hasty retreat. They began adopting a nomadic life-style, but after wandering for eight months they settled briefly on a Texan ranch owned by Berg's former colleague, Fred Jordan. In September 1971, however, Berg again broke with Jordan and like some latter-day Moses led his followers on their resumed exodus.

That event really marked the beginning of The Children of God. The founder began to call himself Moses David and expected his followers also to adopt biblical names. Becoming increasingly autocratic, he expected them to treat him as God's special prophet for the twentieth century, the divinely appointed envoy. He told them his task was to call people to repent, and a major part of that repentance was to reject the churches of Christendom. which he said had turned their backs on Christ and, as predicted in the Book of Revelation, had become part of the great whore of Babylon. He, on the other hand, was God's faithful mouthpiece and his writings, especially his Mo-letters, were the only true and legitimate interpretations of the Bible. With such indoctrination, the Children of God came to see themselves as the only faithful, God-fearing remnant in a God-rejecting world ill-served by a worldly, half-hearted and hypocritical Church.

David Berg died in 1994, after spending the latter years of his life virtually as a recluse during which his followers said he no longer led the movement. Although his outrageous Mo-letters ceased to appear, however, the Good News leaflets which replaced them bore all the hallmarks of Berg's rumbustious style. It remains to be seen whether the movement continues or, like many other cults, it disappears into oblivion with the death of its charismatic leader.

The signs are that it will continue. Members of The Family are still active in the United States, Europe and further afield. In Australia, for example, police and welfare organisations in Sydney and Melbourne have been expressing particular concern about the effect of the cult's unconventional life-style on members' children.

As The Children of God, they were particularly active in Britain in the 1970s but twenty years later seemed to have become a spent force in this country. Now with their new name, The Family, and sometimes describing themselves as the Fellowship of Independent Christian Missionary Communities, they are again working hard to win acceptance as an evangelical Christian group and are making renewed efforts to gain a foothold. Recent reports indicate some Family activity in the London area and around some Oxford colleges, and early in 1994 they were operating from a newly-acquired British headquarters in Duntin Bassett, Leicestershire.

WHAT THE CHILDREN OF GOD BELIEVE

Berg, the World and the Church

The Children of God believe that they are the only true Christians, the only obedient servants of God at work in the world today. Outside the movement everything is sinful, satanical, hypocritical and anti-Christian. In the extravagant language typical of his Mo-letters Berg wrote: 'Kids have been kidnapped from their homes by the laws of compulsory school attendance; drugged to damnation by modern, godless, and useless public education; hypnotised by TV, movies, magazines, and modern music; and imprisoned by modern curfews, child labour laws, parental jurisdiction laws, minimum marriage age laws, minor's laws, and draft regulations and military bondage'.[1]

Berg's followers believe that mainstream Christian churches are as anti-Christian and ungodly as organisations not claiming to be Christian. 'The fiendish, devilish economic system, we hate it, and we teach the kids to hate it, and the False Church system ... We hate the hypocrisy, self-righteousness, lies and deceitfulness of those who claim to be the Church, but are not and we hate the Spiritual system of the Devil behind them.'[2]

Berg taught that, despite their small numbers, God had called the Family to fight on his side against everything evil. Just as Jesus is described as the 'greatest of all Revolutionaries', so too his apostles were his 'twelve bearded militants' who fought with a 'commando-guerrilla type of hit and run tactics'.[3] Members of the Family must follow these examples, for they are today's Christian revolutionaries.

Everything outside their organisation is part of the devil's system and will be destroyed. Those recognising and involved in this evil, godless system are labelled 'systemites' and must be opposed in every way. Such views encourage a persecution complex among members. Not only are these 'systemites' the enemies who must be opposed, but those daring to oppose them must be ready to face suffering at their hands. Persecution is seen as evidence that the Family are right, for it demonstrates that the devil is taking their opposition seriously. It almost seems to be welcomed and cultivated, for persecution encourages a sense of group identity and dependence and makes it all the more difficult for waverers to break away from the cult.

Berg and the Bible

When they first appeared, the Children of God seemed to be simple evangelical Christians with a love for the scriptures which they claimed to regard as the inspired Word of God. Much of their energy was spent encouraging novices to learn Bible texts by heart. It soon became clear, however, that even greater prominence was given to Berg than to the Bible. Members saw Berg as God's special messenger, the prophet for our time, the Lord's spokesman. It followed that the Bible could be interpreted in only one way – Berg's way. In practice, therefore, though lipservice was paid to the Bible, the real authority within the sect was David Berg. As Moses David, he was God's mouthpiece, the sole source of true religion.

That was not all. Berg's role was not merely that of interpreting scripture, for before long he was producing it. His followers came to believe that in Berg's Mo-letters they had what amounted to a continuation of the Bible for today. God was using Moses David to speak to the present generation just as he had used Isaiah, Jeremiah, Ezekiel and others to speak to previous generations. These views still prevail among the members of The Family today.

From the first mainstream Christians have rejected these claims, believing them to be either the meanderings of a man deluded by megalomania or the deliberate deceptions of a religious confidence trickster. The view that Berg's writings are 'inspired' is a hollow claim to those familiar with the Mo-letters. Not only were they written in a racy style and sometimes punctuated with foul language, but they contained a number of explicitly sexual images and in some places descriptions of the sex act itself.

Berg seemed to be completely obsessed by sex. In his defence, members have said their leader was merely emphasising that sex, as a God-given gift, is meant to be enjoyed, not something of which to be ashamed. It is difficult to believe, however, that in trying to make this point Berg needed to go into great detail when describing, for example, his own sexual dreams. More realistically, his writings may be regarded as pornographic.

There is evidence that Berg's own sexual behaviour was not as wholesome as his followers would like us to believe. One of his daughters accused him of attempting an incestuous relationship with her.[4] Nor was such behaviour confined to his own family. In a Channel Four television programme in 1994, people who claimed to be members of the movement were shown making sexually explicit films for Berg's benefit, including one scene of female masturbation, sent to show Berg how much his followers loved him.

Other leaders were not slow to follow Berg's example. The same programme carried interviews with the Pardilla family, all of whom claimed they were raped, sexually abused, or forced unwillingly into sexual relations with Children of God leaders. It was alleged that teenage daughters of Mrs Pardilla were encouraged to take part in striptease sessions for members' entertainment. Debbie Pardilla claimed that from the age of fifteen she was forced to have sex with leaders and that she became pregnant when eighteen and twenty.

Berg, the Second Coming and Judgement

From the start, the Children of God emphasised the Second Coming of Christ, and that emphasis is carried over into its 'Family' phase. Members believe that Christ's Second Coming is imminent and have sometimes gone as far as to predict the year this will occur, 1993 being the most recent failed prediction. This emphasis on an imminent parousia is characteristic, not only of a number of groups on the Christian perimeter, but also of many mainstream Christians. Unlike most orthodox Christians, however, the Family tends to be fairly specific about what they believe will happen when Christ returns. Not only do they speak in general terms about his return as Judge, but they go on to spell out what form that judgement will take and who will suffer under it. In particular they expect severe punishment to be meted out to the churches of the western world and to the materialistic society to which, Berg and his followers claim, the churches have conformed. They, in contrast, expect to be fighting victoriously on God's side against a one-state government of anti-Christ before the end of this decade. In this respect, the Children of God have much in common with Jehovah's Witnesses, though in most respects the two movements are very different.

Motivated by such views, the Family calls people, especially young people, to join God's army as Christ's revolutionaries. Those successfully recruited are expected to forsake all, including families, friends and jobs, since all other people are 'systemites' and all other activities are part of the world of anti-Christ.

CHILDREN OF GOD METHODS

Total control

When new converts join the Family they are required to commit themselves unreservedly to the movement.

The whole of their tightly controlled life now revolves around the colony of members in which they now live. Members are rarely allowed any time out on their own. There is no normal social contact with the outside world. When members are allowed to move out of their base, it is as a group and for the purpose of witnessing and distributing literature. They always work in pairs, younger and more recent converts being supervised by more established members.

In response to this tight control over members, in 1972 some worried American parents formed FREECOG (Parents Committee to Free Our Sons and Daughters from the Children of God) in San Diego. The sect's response was predictable, for they formed THANKCOG, a rival organisation of parents said to be grateful to the movement for the good influence it has exerted over their children.

Outreach

Much of the movement's evangelistic outreach follows a traditional pattern of evangelism, with public witnessing and the distribution of literature (which they call 'litnessing'). But members of the Family are much more committed to, and persistent in, this kind of outreach than are conventional Christians, often spending up to ten hours a day distributing their pamphlets and talking to contacts. Working in public places such as shopping areas, each member has a quota of pamphlets to sell and is expected to spend however many hours it takes to achieve and if possible surpass the set target.

Sometimes more dramatic kinds of outreach take place. Members have been known to dress themselves as prophets of doom, wearing red sackcloth to denote the need to repent and with their foreheads daubed with ash as a sign of mourning. Then, parading publicly with wooden yokes around their necks symbolising bondage, wearing earrings as signs that they are slaves of Christ, and carrying wooden staves signifying judgement, they have interrupted public ceremonies or church services to proclaim God's judgement upon society and to call for repentance.

The philosophy behind such activity is made clear. 'We have declared War of the Spirit on the system's godless schools, Christless churches, and heartless Mammon! We long to return to the Truth, Love, Peace, and Beauty of our Ancients in dress, customs, appearance, and the simple Life of True Happiness in God and love for our fellow man'.[5]

Love-bombing

A great emphasis on what they describe as love has been one of the movement's chief recruiting weapons. Members tell contacts, 'We believe in Jesus and we really love you'. It is all part of the 'love-bombing' technique characteristic of this and some other movements. From reports in the Press it suggestested that some of the Children of God have taken such love bombing to its extreme by offering sex to outsiders, allegedly 'to show them the love of God'. 'Jesus taught that we should be willing to die for others', they argue. 'Surely, then, we ought to be willing to give them sex.'[6] Members have been enjoined to become 'hookers for Jesus'.[7] Permissiveness in sexual morality sometimes includes the exchanging of sexual partners within the movement.[8] It is significant that when asked whether this practice continues in the Family today, members invariably reply that they are not prepared to discus their personal sex life in public. Former members claim that although sex may no longer be on offer to outsiders because of the fear of Aids, the practice of partner-swopping continues within the movement itself.

WHERE THE FAMILY AND MAINSTREAM CHRISTIANS PART COMPANY

The Bible

Like mainstream Christians, members of the movement from its Children of God days to its more recent Family era have always claimed a biblical basis for their teaching. They also say they are fully committed to, and have a living experience of, Jesus Christ as Saviour and Lord. Unlike some of the other sects examined in this book, the Children of God do not reject cardinal Christian doctrines such as the Trinity and the Incarnation, and because of their emphasis on salvation through faith in Christ, as well as the teaching about Christ's second Coming, they are often mistaken for evangelical Christians.

With Berg at their head, their departure from mainstream Christianity was not through rejecting orthodox Christian doctrines, therefore, but through listening uncritically to the views of one man and allowing him to dictate how they were to interpret scripture and therefore to prescribe what they were to believe and how they were to behave. The fundamental point of departure, was in regard to the place they allowed Berg to occupy at the centre of their organisation and the influence they allowed him to have over every aspect of their lives.

For his followers, David Berg's writings and pronouncements have provided at the very least the sole authoritative interpretation of the Bible. In this respect alone they are similar to Christian Scientists who still view Mary Baker Eddy's *Science and Health with Key to the Scriptures* as the only valid interpretation of the Bible's teaching. Like the Mormons, however, The Family have gone further, sometimes treating Berg's writings (as Mormons treat Smith's *Book of Mormon*, *Doctrine and Covenants*, and *Pearl of Great Price*) as additional divine revelations through a modern prophet and, therefore, to some extent as additional scriptures. Claiming to be a Bible-only group they have become in practice a Bible-plus group. In Kurt Hutten's terminology, they are a movement with 'a Bible in the left hand', that is another source of authority which they use to interpret, and often to supplement or supersede, the teaching of the Bible itself.[9]

Parents and Children

A clear example of the way the Family or their Children of God antecedents have slavishly followed Berg particular interpretation of the Bible, is seen with regard to Matthew 10:34-37. Berg persuaded his followers that the passage enjoined converts to forsake parents and break all family ties. The passage certainly shows that Jesus demands a loyalty above all other loyalties. There may well be occasions when even the wishes of close relatives have to take second place because they conflict with what we understand to be the will of God for us. But this is a far cry from the view which seems to imply that an automatic consequence of becoming disciples is that young people must turn their backs on their parents, pausing long enough only to collect from them as much of their money and as many of their material possessions as they can persuade them to part with before they leave. There are, of course, other scriptures stressing the importance of honouring parents and fostering family ties, such as Exodus 20.12 and Ephesians 6.1. Here again, however, the movement relies on Berg's special interpretation to avoid the clear teaching of scripture: obeying parents is re-written as 'obeying your leadership, not your ungodly fleshly parents'.

Sexual behaviour

Berg's preoccupation with sex also needs some comment. Christians have to agree with Berg and his followers that the Christian Church has not always appeared to recognise that sex is a gift of God. But Berg went much further. Instead of stressing the wonder, beauty and sacredness of sexual relationships and the Bible's expectation that they should take place within a life-long marriage bond, Berg's approach was at best coarse and at worst pornographic. When this is allied with the movement's permissiveness and sometimes promiscuity, it raises questions about the reliability of a 'prophet' who persuaded his followers to pursue conduct that was so clearly at variance with the Bible's standards of sexual morality.

By setting up a man as their final authority, by requiring their followers to break natural family ties, by promoting a promiscuous attitude to sex, and by enslaving their followers to a system rather than liberating them to serve Christ freely, the Family, like the Children of God from whom they descended, in my opinion, have demonstrated that their claim to be the only true Christians is hollow.

REFERENCES

1. Mo-Letters.
2. Mo-Letters.
3. Mo-Letters, November 1972.
4. Eileen Barker *New Religious Movements*, pub. HMSO, 1989, page 42 and page 67.
5. Part of a statement signed by recruits.
6. Argued in a 1978 BBC radio programme, 'The Lobster Pot'.
7. Barker op. cit. page 42.
8. Barker op. cit. page 70.
9. Kurt Hutten, *Die Glaubenswelt des Sektierers*, page 104, cited by A. Hoekema, *The Four Major Cults*, page 378.

Chapter 5

THE UNIFICATION CHURCH

Among the many record-breakers listed in *The Guinness Book of Records*, one of the most bizarre is that held by the Korean religious leader, Sun Myung Moon, for the largest number of couples married in a single ceremony. The book's 1994 edition lists 20,825 couples at the Olympic Stadium, Seoul on 25th August 1992, with a further 9,800 couples around the world who took part in the ceremony through a satellite link. Who is Sun Myung Moon? How did his church come into being? What are its beliefs? How do Moon's followers spread those beliefs? These are some of the questions addressed in this chapter.

SUN MYUNG MOON

Sun Myung Moon, founder of the Unification Church, was born on 6th January 1920 in North Korea as one of eight children raised by Presbyterian parents in humble circumstances. Moon claimed that on Easter Day 1936, when he was sixteen years old, he received the first of a series of direct divine revelations. Jesus Christ appeared to him on a Korean mountainside. Christ informed him that he, Moon, was to accomplish a great work, for he was to complete the restoration of mankind started by Jesus himself nearly 2000 years earlier. Thus Christianity would be reborn and in its new Moon-mediated form would embrace people of all Christian denominations.

According to Moon this experience led him to devote himself to intensive Bible study and long hours of prayer. He claims that he was also given many subsequent visions spanning many years, in the course of which he was allowed to converse directly with Old Testament characters such as Abraham, Isaac, Jacob, Moses and Elijah, New Testament personalities like Peter, Paul and John the Baptist, figures from more recent church history such as Wesley, and founders of other world religions including Muhammad, Confucius and the Buddha. In addition to such claims, Moon asserted that he was able to move freely in the spirit realm and had become the medium through which divine revelations reached people living in his day. He was God's special envoy to this disunited twentieth-century world with its competing Christian churches.

During the Second World War Sun Myung Moon studied electrical engineering at Waseda University, Tokyo, though it is not clear whether he ever graduated or went on to use his studies to earn a living. Subsequently, however, he became a successful businessman, building up profitable interests in pharmaceuticals, tuna fish, ginseng tea and air rifles, alongside his religious activities. Before prosperity came to him, however, further revelations in 1945 convinced him that he was the absolute victor of heaven and earth and he adopted his name which means 'shining sun and moon'. He founded the Broad Sea Church of Korea and, at this stage, appears to have been closely associated with an extreme branch of Pentecostalism which believed that Korea was to be the site of the New Jerusalem and the birthplace of the new Messiah.

Meanwhile, in 1948 Moon had been imprisoned by the communists. His followers describe this as a period of bitter persecution for his religious beliefs and he is said to have endured this ordeal with great courage, providing a shining example to his fellow-sufferers. He was released by the advancing United States forces in 1950.

In 1954 Moon founded the Holy Spirit Association for the Unification of World Christianity, now known more simply as the Unification Church. His disciples are often dubbed Moonies. The year 1957 saw the publication of the first edition of *Divine Principle*, probably written by a close associate though outlining Moon's beliefs.

Another significant event in the church's history occurred in 1960, when Moon married Hak-ja Han. Previous marriages had broken up because, so Moon explains, his partners could neither understand or accept his religion. Moon and Hak-ja Han claimed to be the True Parents, and disciples were expected to call them Father and Mother. The couple have produced a large natural family of their own but their followers are said to constitute the Divine Family which in all respects is expected to take precedence over the disciples' own families.

Moon moved from Korea to the United States in 1972, claiming he was told to do so in a further divine revelation, and settled in a mansion on an Irvington, New York estate. From there in 1975 Moon began his world-wide mission, despatching three missionaries to each of ninety-five countries. He and his followers believed that the 1980s would mark the time of the revelation of the Messiah, who would perfect the work begun but not completed by Jesus. The implication was clear, though usually not spelt out by either Moon or his followers: the Messiah would turn out to be none other than Sun Myung Moon himself.

UNIFICATION CHURCH BELIEFS

Sects on the Christian perimeter fall roughly into two categories, those claiming to base their teaching entirely on the Bible, and those claiming additional divine revelation recorded in either extra scriptures or a book providing the only legitimate interpretation of the Bible. The Unification Church belongs to the second of these categories, for its founder is regarded as God's special spokesman and the book *Divine Principle* is thought to be the one interpretation without which the reader will remain blind to the true meaning of the Bible. Although the Bible is frequently quoted in Unification Church publications, as well as by members in their missionary activities, therefore, the real source of the Unification Church's beliefs and practices is Sun Myung Moon.

God's spokesman

Moon's additional truth appears to come largely through clairvoyant and spiritualistic experiences, the most important being the initial vision in which, so Moon claimed, Jesus showed him that he had been selected to accomplish a great mission and to complete the unfinished work of Jesus himself. Therefore, in answer to the question 'With what authority do you teach what you do?', Moon replied, 'I spoke with Jesus Christ in the spirit world. And I spoke also with John the Baptist. This is my authority'.[1] That is how his followers can claim, 'With the fullness of time God sent his messenger to resolve the fundamental questions of life and the universe. His name is Sun Myung Moon'.[2] Moon, therefore, is believed to herald a Golden Age for the human race, himself asserting , 'He (God) is living in me and I am in the incarnation of him'.[3] He tells his followers, 'I am a thinker, I am your brain'.[4]

All of this accords well with other extravagant claims made about Moon within the Unification Church. He is described as 'absolute victor of heaven and earth' and the spirit world is said to have bowed down to him and acknowledged him as Lord of creation, for he has fought against and triumphed over satanic forces.[5] That is why he has become a cult figure to his followers. One described him as 'like the physical representation of God', adding, 'You pray to God, but you pray through our True Parents, Sun Myung Moon and his wife our Mother in the same way that Christians pray through Jesus'.[6]

It is no surprise to discover, therefore, that everything that is distinctive about the Unification Church's beliefs stems directly from Moon himself. For his followers, Moon speaks for God. He alone represents divine authority. That is largely why critics describe Unification Church members as Moonies; and it is not a title to which they object.

The Bible

The Unification Church's most important publication, *Divine Principle*, is claimed to be the sole authoritative interpretation of the Bible. Moon argues strongly for the need of such an interpretation. The Bible, he says, is a book of mystery: it does not use plain language. Indeed, the Bible is presented to us in symbols and parables, so that its real meaning is never obvious. Why does God use such subterfuge? To Moon the answer is simple. 'If God revealed his strategy too openly or plainly, that information would be used by the enemy against God's own champions. That is why the Bible is written as a coded message, so that only God's agents or champions could decipher it – not the enemy.'[7]

It is clear where Moon is leading us. 'If you attempt to interpret the Bible literally, word for word, letter for letter, without understanding the nature of the coded message of the Bible, you are liable to make a great mistake.'[8] But help is at hand. 'God has called me as his instrument to reveal his message for his present-day dispensation, so that there may be a people prepared for the day of the Lord.'[9] This is Moon's justification for teaching that is clearly at variance with what most Bible interpreters would regard as the plain teaching of scripture.

All of this means that, no matter what lip-service is paid to the Bible, within the Unification Church the Bible's authority comes a poor second to that of Sun Myung Moon. Without him to show its true meaning, his followers believe, it is less than adequate as a guide to God's truth for modern men and women. Indeed, those to whom the Bible was first addressed were of low spiritual and intellectual standards compared to people today. Nowadays, however, intelligent men and women can understand the scriptures because in Moon's interpretation all the problems of religion and science are solved. Elsewhere, Moon comes close to admitting that the Unification Church's use of the Bible is little more than a strategic device to help forward the work of proselytising. 'Until our mission with the Christian Church is over, we must quote the Bible and use it to explain the Divine Principle. After we receive the inheritance of the Christian Church, we shall be free to teach without the Bible.'[10]

It is clear, therefore, that far from being biblical, the Unification Church is based entirely on the revelations claimed by Moon. The Bible is then used to support beliefs and practices accepted by the Unification Church on other grounds.

God

Although there is no place within the Unification Church for the Trinity as understood within mainstream Christianity, Unification Church writers have produced their own version of this belief. According to *Divine Principle*, all things – men, animals, plants – exist through the reciprocal relationship of the positive and negative, the subject and the object. Moreover, 'all things' include God, who also exists through a reciprocal relationship between the dual characteristics of positivity and negativity.

Seeking to harmonise this idea with mainstream Trinitarianism, Warren Lewis, Professor of Church History at the Unification Theological Seminary, Barrytown, New York, writes: 'God is triune. In God the Word (Logos) and Wisdom (Holy Spirit) are the perfect expressions of the Father's mind and heart. Word and Wisdom are conceived to be the internal masculine and feminine (yang and yin) duality within God. Hence God's Word and Wisdom are our "True Heavenly Parents".'[11] There is a similar emphasis in *Divine Principle*. 'Jesus was the True Parent of mankind ... He came as the True Father in order to realise the Kingdom of Heaven on earth by giving rebirth to fallen men as children of goodness without original sin ... However, a father alone cannot give birth to children. There must be a True Mother with the True Father, in order to give rebirth to fallen children, as children of goodness. She is the Holy Spirit ... Again, since the Holy Spirit is a female Spirit, we cannot become a "bride" of Jesus unless we receive the Holy Spirit. Thus the Holy Spirit is a female Spirit, consoling and moving the hearts of the people ... She also cleanses the sins of the people in order to restore them, thus indemnifying the sin committed by Eve. Jesus, being male (positivity), is working in heaven, while the Holy Spirit, being female (negativity), is working on earth'.[12]

In a section of *Divine Principle* headed 'Christology', the writer points out several times that Jesus is not God himself. This does not mean simply that Father and Son are distinct persons, with which mainstream Christians would agree. For the Unification Church Jesus is 'the man who has attained the purpose of creation'. As a perfected man, he may be said to 'possess deity' and to have become eternal, but he is not God himself. This in no way denies 'the attitude of faith held by many Christians that Jesus is God, since it is true that a perfected man is one body with God', the writer argues. Moreover, being 'one body with God', Jesus 'may be called a second God (image of God)'.[13]

Moon and his followers categorically deny the deity of Christ. 'Jesus is a man in whom God is incarnate. But he is not God himself', it is asserted.[14] 'Jesus attained deity, as a man who fulfilled the purpose of creation, but can by no means be considered God himself '.[15] Like some of the other sects considered in this book, therefore, the Unification Church, though using some of the language of incarnation, deny the very meaning of incarnation and instead embrace the ancient heresy of adoptionism. The language used here is almost identical with that used by Jehovah's Witnesses in their assertion that Jesus is God with a small 'g'.[16] What is clear is that the deity being ascribed to the Son is different from the Father's deity. Christ's deity is not essential deity: it has been given to him as a reward for his human perfection.

Sin, Sex and Salvation

The First Adam

There is a close connection between sex and sin in Unification Church theology, as Moon and his followers make clear. God created Adam and Eve and placed them in the Garden of Eden, intended that they should marry, have normal sexual relations and as True Parents establish a perfect family on earth. If Adam and Eve had succeeded in this purpose for which they were created, they would have become the true father and mother of all mankind. With the establishment of that true family, a true society, a true nation, and a true world would have come about and God's Kingdom would have been established on earth. Then, following normal physical birth, its members would have passed into the spiritual world where they would have become members of God's spiritual heavenly kingdom and lived eternally in God's love.

Adam and Eve failed to fulfil God's high purpose for them. Eve allowed herself to be sexually seduced by Satan and after that adulterous relationship she proceeded to have normal sexual relations with Adam. Through sexual intercourse, therefore, Adam was involved with Eve in the first sin, and through all subsequent acts of procreation sin infected all Adam's descendants. Thus the first Adam failed as God's agent of salvation.

Moon interprets the Fall in two parts, spiritual and physical. 'Since God created man in spirit and flesh', it is asserted, 'the fall also took place in spirit and flesh. The fall through the blood relationship between the angel and Eve was the spiritual fall, while that through the blood relationship between Eve and Adam was the physical fall.' How Eve, a physical being, could be sexually seduced by Satan, a fallen angelic being, is explained in *Divine Principle*. Feelings and sensations 'are felt and responded to in the invisible, or spirit world. Contact between a spirit and an earthly man (who has a spirit) is not very different from contact between two earthly human beings. Therefore, sexual union between a human being and an angel is actually possible'.[17]

The Second Adam

Like orthodox Christians, members of the Unification Church believe that God sent Jesus to be the Saviour of the world, but they differ from Christians about the way salvation was to be achieved. According to Moon, Jesus, the Second Adam, was meant to accomplish all that the First Adam failed to achieve. God's plan was that the Second Adam should find and marry his perfect 'Eve', produce children, and in that way begin to establish the true family, the true society, the true nation, and the true world. Thereby God's Kingdom would come on earth. Once again, however, the divine plan was frustrated, this time because Jesus was crucified before he could find the ideal wife and get married.

In Unification Church theology, therefore, the Cross is regarded as a disaster. Moon and his followers do not believe that by his death and resurrection Jesus did all that was necessary for human salvation. They acknowledge that the death and resurrection of Jesus has achieved 'spiritual' salvation, but go on to maintain that full salvation – that is physical as well as spiritual salvation – will be achieved only when God's chosen saviour contracts an ideal marriage and begins to establish the God-centred family. 'Redemption through the cross cannot completely liquidate our original sin ... it leaves man's original nature not yet perfectly restored.'[18] In the final analysis, therefore, the mission of Jesus failed because the crucifixion, precipitated by the unwise preaching of John the Baptist, frustrated God's plan of salvation. It then became necessary for God to take further action.

The Lord of the Second Advent

According to *Divine Principle*, God's chosen agent for this further action for human salvation is the Lord of the Second Advent, a Third Adam. The first and second Adam failed to achieve God's purpose, the first because of his sin and the second because of his crucifixion. The Third Adam will succeed, however, by achieving the required perfect marriage, producing the perfect children, and laying the foundation for God's perfect family on earth. This perfect family will consist, not only of the Lord of the Second Advent's own natural children, but all others who align themselves with him and begin to develop a 'heart of God' through loving God and each other perfectly. They will be the new humanity.

Christians will wish to know how these ideas relate to the traditional Christian views of Jesus's Messiahship and Second Coming. The Unification Church's Professor of Church History attempts to explain. 'In our day...Jesus has caused the office of Messiahship to be transferred from himself to the Lord of the Second Advent ... The spirit world ... is working mightily in co-operation with the earthly plane to restore, recreate, and resurrect the entirety of human race in a Kingdom of Heaven on earth.'[19] Moreover, Jesus has not only transferred his role of Messiah to this Third Adam but also, claims Lewis, will 'come again' in the Lord of the Second Advent. The crucial question with which the whole human race is faced, therefore, is: Who is the new Messiah, this Lord of the Second Advent?

The founder of the Unification Church has refrained from making a public bid for this role, though he does not discourage his followers from making this deduction. They appear to be fully convinced that Sun Myung Moon is the new saviour. Thus Lewis writes, 'The Unification Church believes that when all the conditions have been met, it will be Sun Myung Moon whom Jesus has chosen to 'come again' and establish the divine-human family where God and mankind can dwell together in mutual delight'. Cautiously, he adds the caveat, 'But Revd. Moon told me just recently, "If someone assassinates me, God has someone else to do the job".'[20] Lewis adds, 'There is, nevertheless, a "not yet" within Unification eschatology. Though it has a messianic vision and hope, it does not proclaim Moon as Messiah.'

The founder's immediate subordinates prefer designations like 'our Leader', 'our Master', 'Prophet' and 'True Parent'. So 'Moon at this time is only proleptically the "Lord of the Second Advent" ... He is in a state of becoming ... "Messiah-designate". Though he may already function emotionally and religiously as True Father for many church members, he is not actually nor technically the Lord of the Second Advent at this time.' Nevertheless, 'He is a charismatic seer and visionary who has, reportedly, not only visited the spirit world but has won cosmically significant victories there ... Moon is revered as an infallible seer, revelator and prophet'.[21] This Messiah will not come in the clouds as many Christians have mistakenly believed, but will be born on earth in the flesh. He will appear in Korea. The conclusion, though never stated publicly, is clear to members of the Unification Church. Sun Myung Moon, born in Korea in 1920, is the Lord of the Second Advent, the twentieth-century manifestation of the Christ. So 'the marriage of the

lamb prophesied in the 19th chapter of Revelation took place in 1960 ...
Thus the Lord of the Second Advent and His Bride became the True
Parents of mankind'.[22]

UNIFICATION CHURCH METHODS

One of the chief difficulties confronting anyone concerned with the activities of the Unification Church is the large number of names under which
this movement operates. As well as its more specific activities, it sponsors
a number of international cultural and scientific conferences. These
'extra-church' activities help to create for the church and its leaders an air
of academic and social respectability.

Among the many groups operating under the general umbrella of the
Unification Church, some of the most significant are the International
Federation for Victory over Communism (VOC), the Freedom Leader-
ship Foundation (FLF), the Collegiate Association for Research Principles
(CARP), and the International Cultural Foundation.

Alongside all of this, there is the direct proselytising work of Moon's
rank and file disciples. They are some of the most disarmingly charming
missionaries. Whether the first contact is on a street corner, in a shopping
complex, at a railway station, or in some other public place, potential
converts are always greeted with a smile and a warm invitation to support
some 'good cause' by purchasing a magazine, flowers, or some other
cheap object.

Missionaries generally do not reveal their true identity at this stage of
the encounter or to point out the specific beliefs they hold. Often there is
little indication that their movement is religious, there is no mention of
Sun Myung Moon, and they have been known to deny their membership
of the Unification Church.

If contacts show more than polite interest, they may be invited to a
meal with local church members, to an evening lecture, or even to a three-
day house party or conference. Whatever form the follow-up takes,
potential converts find themselves subjected to a combination of exces-
sive and exuberant demonstrations of loving concern and a well-prepared
verbal onslaught calculated to wear down their resistance and to persuade
them to stay for more. Even at this stage, Unification Church members
do not readily admit their allegiance.

Eventually, however, potential converts are persuaded to make a
commitment to the movement, but it should not be thought that this is
like any other religious conversion experience. Here converts are
expected to obey their Unification Church superiors without question, to

give up thinking for themselves, and to make a complete break with the secular world which, so they are taught, is completely in the hands of Satan. Such a break may also include their closest relatives. Their commitment will mean being ready to work unceasingly for the Unification Church, their tasks ranging from the most menial tasks within the local church commune to up to twenty hours a day peddling the movement's goods to raise as much money as possible from the unsuspecting and gullible public. There is much well-documented evidence from former Unification Church members of the effect of these methods on people who are persuaded to join the Unification Church.

WHERE THE UNIFICATION CHURCH AND MAINSTREAM CHRISTIANITY PART COMPANY

UNIFICATION CHURCH	CHRISTIANITY
The Bible	
The Bible is written in coded language and its meaning is accesible only to Moon and those who follow his teaching. In practice this means that his extra-biblical statements are also regarded as God-given truths.	God has revealed all that he wants us to know of himself and his will for us in Christ, his incarnate Word, through the Bible, his written word. The Bible is the norm by which all claims to religious truths are to be measured, including those of religious leaders claiming special powers of interpretation.
God	
The world's True Parents are God himself (the Father) and the Holy Spirit (the Mother)	God is trinity, Father, Son, and Holy Spirit, three co-equal and co-eternal divine Persons in the unity of the Godhead

UNIFICATION CHURCH	CHRISTIANITY
Jesus Christ	
Though he is not God in the full sense, Jesus Christ is the Second Adam raised up by God. His mission was to save mankind by forming the Perfect Family. His mission failed because he died on the cross before that task was completed. God therefore raised up another Saviour, the Lord of the Second Advent (Sun Myung Moon) to do what Jesus failed to achieve.	As the one who is both God and Man, Jesus was sent by his Father to reveal God to us and to die on the cross to save us. By his death and the vindication of his resurrection, Jesus has done all that is necessary for our salvation. There is no need for another Saviour.
Salvation	
This is obtained when human beings allow themselves to become adopted members of Sun Myung Moon's family by becoming his disciples. Mr Moon and his wife then become the disciple's earthly father and mother, just as the Father and the Holy Spirit are his or her Heavenly Parents.	God's gift of salvation is offered to all by grace and is appropriated through faith in Christ. Those who respond in faith die to sin and rise to new life in Christ, as symbolised in Baptism.
The Church	
Though claiming to be a movement for the unification of world-wide Christianity, the Unification Church denies much of what the mainstream Churches affirm. It has set up a rival church in opposition to the mainstream Churches.	The one Church consists of all who through faith have received Jesus as Saviour and acknowledge him as Lord. Despite their denominational barriers, the mainstream Churches share the apostolic faith.

REFERENCES

1. Speech at New Orleans, Louisiana, 28th October 1973.
2. *Divine Principle* (pub. Holy Spirit Association for the Unification of World Christianity, 1973) page 36.
3. *New Hope*, page 36.
4. Master Speaks, 17th May 1973.
5. *Divine Principle*, page 16.
6. Rosalind Mitchell in 'Farewell to the Cults', *Crusade* 20th January 1978.
7. Sun Myung Moon, *The New Future of Christianity* (pub. Holy Spirit Association for the Unification of World Christianity, 1974) pages 83f.
8. ibid page 86.
9. ibid.
10. *Master Speaks* March/April 1965 page 1.
11. Warren Lewis in *A Time for Consideration* (ed. Bryant and Richardson, pub. The Edwin Mellen Press, New York 1978) page 194.
12. *Divine Principle*, pages 214f.
13. ibid pages 209–211.
14. Young Oon Kim, *The Divine Principle and its Application* (pub. The Holy Spirit Association for the Unification of World Christianity).
15. *Divine Principle*, page 28.
16. see pages 81–83 and 91.
17. *Divine Principle*, page 77.
18. ibid page 142.
19. Warren Lewis in *A Time for Consideration*, page 187.
20. ibid.
21. Lewis, op cit. page 197.
22. *The Divine Principle and its Application*, page 196.

Chapter 6

CHRISTIAN SCIENTISTS

On 1st February 1866, a forty-five year old American woman, who had suffered years of illness, fell on the ice near Lynn, Massachusetts, and received injuries which left her unable to walk. Lying helpless in bed, she asked for a Bible and, turning to Matthew 9, read the story of Jesus healing the paralysed man. She said that, as she reflected on this miracle, she became aware of God's truth, was freed from all pain and, like the man in the story, was completely healed and left her bed and walked. As a result of that experience, she went on to become founder of the Christian Science Church and its international newspaper, *The Christian Science Monitor*, and author of Christian Science's textbook, *Science and Health with Key to the Scriptures*.

THE FOUNDER OF CHRISTIAN SCIENCE

The woman concerned was Mary Baker Eddy. The youngest of six children, she was born into a Congregationalist home in a farming community at Bow, New Hampshire, in 1821. Family life was characterised by daily prayer and Bible reading. Sundays were given over to church activities. The family home became a place of constant theological debate, as her father offered hospitality to a string of Christian preachers. Mary was often an interested but silent listener to these conversations, which contributed to her developing spirituality. In her teens, however, she began to rebel against her father's strict Calvinistic views. She was especially resentful of the view that God might predestine some to salvation and others to damnation, her to heaven and her brothers to hell, so she began to embark on a search for other religious patterns.

Mary married her first husband, George Glover, in 1843 and moved with him to Charleston, South Carolina. Tragically, she was widowed within a year, when he died of yellow fever. She returned to her New Hampshire family home, where her son, George, was born shortly afterwards. Certain domestic difficulties and her own deteriorating health resulted in her son being unofficially adopted by a friend's family when he was seven, and mother and son drifted apart.

Mary's second marriage, to a dentist named Daniel Patterson, occurred in 1853, but this proved a failure. Patterson turned out to be an unstable character who was unable to support his wife and was unfaithful to her. She divorced him in 1873 for desertion.

Some ten years earlier she had met Phineas Quimby, a healer who focused on an approach to healing through the mind. Quimby believed that in approaching sickness in this way he had rediscovered the secret of Jesus' healing ministry. Mary Patterson, as she then was, benefited briefly from this treatment, but then Quimby himself died in 1866. Afterwards, her religious opponents claimed that much of her Christian Science teaching had been derived from Quimby. Christian Scientists have always denied this, claiming that their respective views were very different.

Then in 1866 she had the healing experience that was to transform her life and lead her to become the Founder and (as she preferred to say) Discoverer of Christian Science. Years later she wrote, 'That short experience included a glimpse of the great fact that I have since tried to make plain to others, namely, Life in and of Spirit; this Life being the sole reality of existence'.[1]

Although controversy has always surrounded this event, with the evidence as to the seriousness of her injuries and their likely outcome never being conclusive, there can be little doubt that a remarkable change took place in Mary Baker Eddy herself. 'This incident seems to have marked a redirection in her life, impelling several years of intense scriptural study and writing, together with further healing experiences through which she tested her developing conclusions'.[2] As her thinking continued to crystallise, she felt she had to relinquish many entrenched assumptions about materiality and to think spiritually. She was led to see 'the allness of God and the nothingness of evil; the allness of Spirit and the nothingness of matter; the spiritual character and perfection of God's creation; and the demonstrable possibilities of these propositions as fundamental Truth'.[3] As she wrote, 'My discovery that erring, mortal, misnamed *mind* produces all the organism and action of the mortal body, set my thoughts to work in new channels, and led up to my demonstration of the proposition that Mind is All and matter is naught as the leading factor in Mind-science'.[4]

THE CHRISTIAN SCIENCE TEXTBOOK

Mary Baker Eddy published the first edition of the Christian Science textbook, *Science and Health with Key to the Scriptures*, in 1875. For the next thirty-five years she continued to work on its contents, making some major revisions before giving the book its final form. Just before her death in December 1910, she took legal steps to ensure that only The Bible and *Science and Health with Key to the Scriptures* were to be read at all Christian Science church services. There was to be no preaching or exposition. In keeping with that requirement, Christian Science churches have two lecterns, one holding the Bible and the other *Science and Health with Key to the Scripture*. Services focus on the reading of sections from each, as directed by the Church's Boston headquarters, a practice which helps to maintain uniformity of belief and practice among Christian Scientists and eliminates the possibility of private interpretations by members or deviations by leaders.

Like the Mormon Church, therefore, Christian Science, although affirming the importance of the Bible, looks to another inspired and authoritative written source for its beliefs and practices. Christian Scientists do not go quite as far as Mormons in claiming that their textbook is the Word of God. Nevertheless, they do assert that *Science and Health with Key to the Scriptures* is the one true interpretation of the Bible's message. What this means in practice is that *Science and Health*, though not called scripture, is treated as if it were scripture. The Bible is read in the light of the Christian Science textbook and no interpretations of the Bible are allowed other than those already prescribed by Mary Baker Eddy.

A Christian Science writer explains that 'for an understanding of God, the Christian Scientist turns to two textbooks he considers authoritative. The first is the Bible.' That writer goes on to say that 'the Bible occupies a unique place; it records the unfolding revelation of the nature of God. It contains within its pages the way of salvation.' Turning to *Science and Health with Key to the Scriptures* he added, 'In no way does this textbook replace the Bible. The phrase *Key to the Scriptures* indicates the relationship'.[5] A little later, however, he appears to depart from what seems a traditional Christian view. 'God is known only through revelation. And the Scientist finds his revelation to be recorded in the inspired teachings of the Scriptures **and** *Science and Health*'.[6]

That writer was merely stating what Mary Baker Eddy herself claimed and what all her followers have believed ever since. Although they are ready to affirm, 'As adherents of Truth, we take the inspired Word of the Bible as our sufficient guide to eternal life',[7] they are equally quick to speak of 'the presence of the Word of God, present not only in the Bible, but also in this remarkable textbook',[8] Mary Baker Eddy had clearly pointed her followers in this direction, claiming in her book *Miscellany*, 'It was not myself, but the divine power of Truth and Love, infinitely above me, which dictated *Science and Health with Key to the Scriptures* ...

I should blush to write of the book as I have, were it of human origin, and were I, apart from God, its author. But, as I was only a scribe echoing the harmonies of heaven in divine metaphysics, I cannot be super-modest in my estimate of the Christian Science textbook'.[9]

No one could accuse Mary Baker Eddy of super-modesty, for this last statement comes close to claiming for *Science and Health* what extreme biblical fundamentalists claim for the Bible, namely that it was written at God's dictation. The Christian Science movement stands or falls, therefore, on the contents of the Christian Science textbook, for *Science and Health with Key to the Scriptures* is not just a contribution to an understanding of Christian Science: it *is* Christian Science.

THE CHRISTIAN SCIENCE CHURCH

The Mother Church and its Branch Churches

The Church of Christ, Scientist was founded four years after the publication of the first edition of *Science and Health*. Eddy had taught her first class in 1870 and began to attract a following in Lynn, Massachusetts. At first she believed that, because Christian Science was so self-evidently true, it would command itself to the established churches and they would accept it and allow it to transform their beliefs and practices. Very soon, however, she was facing opposition on three counts: first social – she was a woman in a male dominated society; secondly, ecclesiastical – she was unorthodox in her beliefs; thirdly, medical – her views denied the fundamentals upon which medical practice was built. In 1879, therefore, she agreed with fifteen of her supporters to 'organize a church designed to commemorate the word and works of our Master, which should reinstate primitive Christianity and its lost element of healing'.[10] So like Charles Taze Russell of the Jehovah's Witnesses, Joseph Smith of the Mormons, John Thomas of the Christadelphians, and the leaders of other nineteenth century alternatives to mainstream Christianity, Mrs Eddy claimed to be recalling the Church to its first century roots.

At first the growth of her Church was anything but spectacular, but the momentum increased through Christian Science healings in the Boston area. Eddy had established the Massachusetts Metaphysical College in Boston in 1881, and although it was closed in 1889, the work done by Eddy and her students in those eight years had a dramatic effect on the Church's growth. Eddy was pastor of the central Boston Church until 1890 and the local churches which it spawned appointed their own pastors. Anxious that some of the teaching from some of these churches did not always reflect her views, however, in 1895 Eddy ordered that in future there would be two impersonal pastors in all her churches, the Bible and *Science and Health with Key to the Scriptures*, a practice which has continued to the present day.

To tighten her control still further, Mrs Eddy renamed her first church, The Mother Church, The First Church of Christ, Scientist, and ordered that in future all other Christian Science churches were to be branch churches of the mother church. Despite some schisms and defections, Christian Science continued to grow, especially between 1920 and 1930.

Although there is evidence of some decline since then, there are now about 3,000 branch churches societies and college organizations in over fifty countries. Branch churches are formed where there are no fewer than sixteen Christian Scientists, societies are smaller groups, and Christian Scientists in universities and colleges establish themselves as organizations. Though democratic in character, all branch churches have strong links with the Mother Church, and conform to the rules set out in Mary Baker Eddy's *Church Manual*.

Membership

According to Bryan Wilson, by 1902 there were about 24,000 Christian Scientists, their number including a few American judges, some businessmen, a number of converted ministers from mainstream Christian denominations, and, surprisingly, a few medical doctors.[11] Four years later the number had grown to over 65,000, by 1926 it had increased to around 270,000, and after that there was a steady, if less spectacular, growth in membership. Although it is no longer possible to be accurate about numbers because the movement does not publish membership statistics, its current world membership is probably between 350,000 and 450,000, of whom there are probably about 50,000 British Christian Scientists.

Like many mainstream Churches, Christian Science has seen a fall in numbers in recent years. An eminent sociologist suggests reasons for the decline. Christian Science has not fulfilled its early promise to transform medical practice and treatment and now has to contend with widely accepted theories concerning psychosomatic illness which explain most Christian Science cures. The Christian Science Church is also cast unalterably in its founder's mould, its textbook, *Science and Health with Key to the Scriptures*, sounds increasingly dated, and the straitjacket in which Christian Science finds itself makes it impossible for it to adapt to the end of the twentieth century. It has also lost its novelty value, because it is no longer unusual to find a woman in a position of leadership or a religious movement with an emphasis on healing.[12]

The Christian Science Church is largely middle-class, and there is a preponderance of women. 'Manual workers, factory workers, the poor and the uneducated are not drawn into Christian Science' because it 'demands something of a willingness to attribute poverty to the wrong set of mental attitudes'.[13] Another reason may be that the poorer and less educated people are not normally attracted to a movement demanding the intellectual gymnastics of Christian Science philosophy. 'Those of very limited education would find the system incomprehensible because of the plethora of abstract ideas, the extended use of syllogism, the complexity of the argument, the seeming conflict of the teaching with common sense ... and the profusion of multi-syllabic words'.[14] These reasons seem more plausible than an official Christian Science one, that poor and uneducated people have joined the Church but have been transformed as they have embraced its teaching. Their religion 'has moved from their lives the causes of their poverty: ill-health, alcoholism, lack of opportunity, inferiority, insecurity, resignation, personality problems'.[15]

Church Buildings

Christian Science congregations normally meet in fairly plain buildings. There is little in the way of decoration except two short quotations, one from the bible and the other from Mary Baker Eddy, on the wall behind the platform. Usually there are other church rooms on the same site, one of which may be the Christian Science Reading Room, though this is sometimes located in a more prominent place in the local community as part of the local church's outreach to those who are not members. Christian Scientists use their buildings only for strictly religious purposes. Social occasions and money raising activities like fetes, fairs or sales, are avoided. These buildings are not even used for Christian Science marriages, for on such occasions Christian Scientists normally ask ministers of other church denominations to officiate.

Sunday Services

The focal point of a Christian Science service is the reading of the set Lesson-Sermon provided by the Church's Boston headquarters. This Lesson-Sermon consists of a selection of Bible readings from the Authorised Version, together with interpretive passages from *Science and*

Health. The readings follow one of a number of themes used in rotation. The importance of the Lesson-Sermon is emphasised in the way it is introduced: 'The Bible and the Christian Science textbook are our only preachers. We shall now read scriptural texts and their correlative passages from our denominational textbook; these comprise our sermon.' The Lesson-Sermon is then presented without comment by two officially recognized Readers, one of whom presides over the whole service. The service also includes a sacred song performed by a female soloist, congregational hymns, silent prayer, and the Lord's Prayer.

Christian Scientists make no sacramental use of bread, wine, water, or any other material substances in their services, which have been described as Quaker-like in their simplicity. In what appears to be another deliberate attempt to treat the material as illustory and to spiritualise it away, 'the sacraments are conceived of as a process of continuing purification and quiet communion with God'.[16]

Wednesday Testimony Meetings

As on Sundays, the programme for these regular midweek meetings has readings from the Bible and *Science and Health*, hymns, and silent prayer. The most significant feature of these evenings, however, is the second half of the programme which is given over to members' testimonies which are meant to demonstrate the outworkings of Christian Science in everyday life. As we should expect from a movement founded by Mary Baker Eddy on the basis of her own transforming healing experience, stories of healings figure prominently at this meeting and sometimes find their way into the movement's literature for wider publicity. The evidence for healings is largely anecdotal.

Church Organization

At its outset Christian Science had its pastors and teachers, like traditional Christian Churches. Mary Baker Eddy was pastor of the foundational Boston church and other pastors cared for those local churches which developed as the movement grew. As we have seen, however, Mrs Eddy quickly became disillusioned with her fellow pastor/preachers, because they could not always be trusted to preach what she regarded as authentic Christian Science. She therefore decided to remove them from their posts and to replace them with two 'impersonal pastors', the Bible and *Science and Health with Key to the Scriptures*. Perhaps unconsciously she was preparing her followers for her death, and for that stronger bureaucratic control which would replace her charismatic leadership and which would ensure that Christian Science was retained in its Mary Baker Eddy form. During the last twenty years of her life Eddy was building up an impersonal system of control. Pastors gave way to Readers whose period of office was limited to three years. Local churches became branch churches of the Boston Mother Church and were expected to follow its Manual. And although she appointed a Board of Directors, the board was under her control and subject to her veto.

Christian Science has no ordained clergy and encourages the full participation in church life of all its members. Two **Readers** are elected from each branch church's membership to serve for a period of three years. As explained earlier, these key people figure prominently in Sunday services, leading the service and presenting the lesson-sermon. Between five and ten people (the total being determined by the size of the congregation) are elected to serve as the church's **executive board**. Each branch church also has its Christian Science **practitioners**. Listed monthly in the movement's *Christian Science Journal*, they devote themselves full time to a ministry of healing using Christian Science methods. They are the nearest Christian Science comes to the professional ministers of a number of other churches.

Provided they obtain the support of the rest of the congregation, members of a branch church can serve in any church office. Each has an equal voice in the church's decision-making. Because of this, Christian Science prides itself on the democratic manner in which it operates, with each branch church having a measure of local autonomy.

What has to be remembered, however, is that in matters of Christian Science belief, practice and policy, authority is very definitely located in the Mother Church, and this means in effect that Mary Baker Eddy still holds a tight, if posthumous, control over the movement she founded. The **Church Manual** she produced remains a very powerful document for the whole movement and serves as a constitution for all Christian Science churches. The Manual is 'the symbol of Mrs Eddy's achievement as the Founder of Christian Science and the means through which her leadership of the church organisation is perpetuated'.[17] It sets out the basic goals of the church, provides its governmental framework, and guides members about their responsibility and accountability.

The Boston Headquarters

Administrative responsibility for the world-wide Christian Science movement is in the hands of a five-member **Board of Directors**, who themselves fill any vacancies arising in their membership. The Board's purpose is to preserve the authentic teachings of Christian Science, to publish Mary Baker Eddy's writings and, through its Publishing Society, to make available various Christian Science periodicals like the monthly *Journal*, the weekly *Sentinel*, and the *Christian Science Quarterly* containing the Lesson-Sermons. The *Christian Science Monitor*, founded as a Boston daily newspaper in 1908 but now attracting 150,000 readers throughout the world, is another of the Board's responsibilities.

The Board of Directors has an important educational role in the movement. Every three years it is responsible for the more intensive training in Christian Science fundamentals of thirty experienced Christian Science practitioners gathered from all over the world. Graduates from this high-powered course return home to run annual two-week classes in which thirty others are trained. The Boston headquarters also has a Board of Lectureship, consisting of some twenty-eight people who undertake lecture tours throughout the world. The Committee on Publication is run by a manager in Boston but has several thousand representatives in many countries. Each state, province or country where there are Christian Science branches has its own Committee, usually consisting of one person.

CHRISTIAN SCIENCE BELIEFS

REALITY AND UNREALITY

Mary Baker Eddy's belief system has often been described as idealistic. Idealism, a school of philosophy holding that spirit or mind are the fundamental reality, takes two main forms. Objective Idealists take a common sense view of reality, believing that material objects exist, whereas Subjective Idealists believe that material objects have no independent existence of their own but exist only in the minds of those who perceive them. Although her followers deny this, Mrs Eddy was basically a Subjective Idealist. She propounded as the fundamental doctrine of Christian Science that the only reality is Spirit and that the material world and all that goes with it is an illusion or mirage, existing only in what she labelled 'mortal mind'.

'All reality is in God and His creation, harmonious and eternal. That which He creates is good, and He makes all that is made. Therefore the only reality of sin, sickness, or death is the awful fact that unrealities seem real to human, erring unbelief, until God strips off their disguise. They are not true, because they are not of God. We learn in Christian Science that all inharmony of mortal mind is illusion, possessing neither reality nor identity though seeming to be real and identical'.[18]

Christian Science turns to modern physics to support its views, pointing out that physicists believe matter can only be understood math-ematically. The Christian Scientist goes further, however, regarding Spirit as true substance. The movement's healings are cited as evidence of this surpassing power, Christian Science.[19] They claim that their asser-tion about the unreality of matter 'no more denies the existence of humankind or natural objects than the challenge posed in physics to conventional views of perception and to the substantiality of matter denies the existence of the universe'.[20]

This whole argument hinges, of course, on what Eddy meant by 'real' and whether today's Christian Scientists mean the same thing. Taken at their face value, Eddy's statements on the subject seem capable of only one interpretation. The only reality is Spirit – God – the All in All. Material existence does not exist, except in the unenlightened mortal mind of men and women. Contemporary Christian Scientists try to explain her teach-ings in ways that makes more sense, pointing out that 'unreal' and 'real' have a distinct meaning in Christian Science. 'Real' relates only to what is *divinely* true, so when *Science and Health* refers to sickness and sin as 'unreal', it is not saying they are non-existent or unreal in a *human* sense. Christian Scientists say they are simply following Paul's teaching in the New Testament that 'what is seen is transient, what is unseen is eternal'.[21] They believe that from a *divine* standpoint sin is as 'unreal' to God as 'three threes are ten' is unreal to mathematical principle.

It should be noted that in arguing their case Christian Scientists draw a distinction between existence and reality not found in the Bible. Paul's words in 2 Corinthians do not deny the reality of the temporal, but rather affirm it. He goes on to state in the following chapter that 'if the earthly frame that houses us today is demolished, we possess a building which God has provided – a house not made by human hands, eternal and in heaven'.[22] Looking at Paul's words in their context, therefore, it is clear that he has no doubt about the reality of the material. His point is, not that the physical body is unreal, but that though real it is transient, and that one day what is real but transient will give way to what is both real and eternal.

THE BIBLE AND THE CHRISTIAN SCIENCE TEXTBOOK

The first of Christian Science's six tenets states, 'As adherents of Truth, we take the inspired Word of the Bible as our sufficient guide to eternal life'. Though claiming biblical authority for its beliefs, however, Christian Science is entirely dependent upon the teachings of its founder set out once and for all in *Science and Health with Key to the Scriptures*. Nothing can be added to or taken from what Christian Scientists regard as a textbook for all times. The affirmation of the sufficiency of the Bible's teaching has to be understood in the light of the additional fact that the only interpretations of biblical passages allowed in the movement are those of Mary Baker Eddy set out in *Science and Health with Key to the Scriptures*. Everything in the Founder's 1910 revision of that book is unquestioned and unalterable today: it *is* Christian Science.

As we examine other Christian Science beliefs, we shall see that they all spring from Eddy's idealistic philosophical base and that in *Science and Health with Key to the Scriptures* the Bible is interpreted to fit it.

GOD

Divine Principle

Mary Baker Eddy asserted, 'The starting point of divine Science is that God, Spirit, is All-in-all, and there is no other might nor Mind, – that God is Love, and therefore He is divine Principle. To grasp the reality and order of being in its Science, you must begin by reckoning God as the divine Principle of all that really is. Spirit, Life, Truth, Love, combine as one, – and are the Scriptural names for God ... All is Mind and ... Mind is God, omnipotence, omnipresence, omniscience'.[23]

Spiritual Creation

Because of her belief that the only reality is Spirit and that the material world and all that goes with it is an illusion or mirage, Mrs Eddy rejected the traditional Christian view of God as the Creator of the physical world and in particular with that understanding of the Genesis accounts which, taken at their face value, supports the traditional view. She avoided the obvious teaching of Genesis 1 by explaining that it referred to spiritual, not material, creation and exhorted her followers to 'look away from the opposite supposition that man is created materially'.[24]

Eddy devoted almost sixty pages of her textbook to a reinterpretation of Genesis in a rather forced attempt to make this point by spiritualising the text. So creation was not the bringing into existence of physical creatures, but 'the unfolding of spiritual ideas and their identities, which are embraced in the infinite Mind and forever reflected', the 'highest ideas' being 'the sons and daughters of God'.[25] The sun of Genesis 1.16 was not a physical body but 'a metaphorical representation of Soul outside the body, giving existence and intelligence to the universe'.[26] Similarly, the earth's rocky surface stood for 'solid and grand ideas', animals, spiritually interpreted, represented 'the gradation of mortal thought', whilst the birds were 'aspirations soaring beyond and above corporeality to the understanding of the incorporeal and divine Principle, Love'.[27]

Eddy explained that human beings regarded all these things as material, rather than spiritual, because they were as yet unenlightened by Christian Science and still governed by the errors of 'mortal mind'. But such erroneus misconceptions could be put right through her teachings, for, 'when we subordinate the false testimony of the corporeal senses to the facts of Science, we shall see this true likeness and reflection everywhere'. We should then come to see the truth of 'man and woman as coexistent and eternal with God' and reflecting forever 'the infinite Father-Mother God'.[28] She rejected Genesis 2 as 'false history in contradistinction to the truth' and asserted that 'In this erroneous theory, matter takes the place of Spirit. Matter is represented as the life-giving principle of the earth'.[29]

A contemporary presentation of Christian Science acknowledges that this is a radical departure from mainstream Christianity. 'What other Christians do not share is Christian Science's conviction that God is absolutely not the author of the conditions of finitude – meaning material existence – which give rise to suffering and disease. This may well be the most significant non-negotiable difference between Christian Science and traditional Christian theology.' The material world, which people wrongly conclude to be what God created, is an illusion, 'the way creation appears within the habitual limits of human perception'.[30]

Pantheism

Because of such views, Mrs Eddy has sometimes been accused of Pantheism, the belief that God is All and All is God. Forms of Pantheism found in the Hindu tradition hold that there is a unified divine Principle, an infinite reality behind the illusory and imperfect world of perception. Within the Jewish-Christian tradition, the tension held between God's transcendence and his immanence has proved, in general, a solid defence against Pantheism. The seventeenth century philosopher, Benedictus Spinoza, however, who was born a Jew but became a pantheist, said 'Whatever is, is in God'. Without God nothing could be conceived. To talk of God or Nature, therefore, was to talk of the same thing.[31]

Eddy actually argued against Pantheism, which she defined in a more limited way as the belief that there is mind in matter. She said that every system of human philosophy, doctrine, and medicine was infected with this kind of pantheism, for they all believed there was mind in matter. Her point was quite different. There were not two bases of being, matter and mind, but one alone – Mind, God. Many would see this as coming perilously close to Pantheism. She was certainly not far removed from the Hindu concept that the only reality is Ultimate Reality and that all separate existences are an illusion. In describing God as All, she ruled out what a sympathetic commentator has called 'the legitimacy, permanence and substantiality of anything contrary to God's nature'.[32]

Unlike the more thoroughgoing pantheists, however, Eddy was also ready to speak of God in personal terms. Whereas they believed that God was impersonal Principle, she was sometimes happy to describe God as Father, or even, more radically for her day, as Father-Mother.[33] At other times she seemed more at home with impersonal titles like 'Principle; Mind; Soul; Spirit; Life; Truth; Love; all substance; intelligence'.[34] She advised caution in the use of 'person' and 'personality' when applied to God because of the linguistic ambiguity and therefore confusion involved. 'As the words *person* and *personality* are commonly and ignorantly applied, they often lead, when applied to Deity, to confused and erroneous conceptions of divinity and its distinction from humanity. If the term personality, as applied to God, means infinite personality, then God is infinite *Person* ... An infinite Mind in a finite form is an absolute impossibility'.[35] No matter how God was described, however, Eddy had no doubt that he alone was to be worshipped. There may be doubts about whether her philosophy was idealistic and bordering on the pantheistic, but there can be no misunderstanding about her theology: it was very definitely unitarian.

THE TRINITY

Like leaders of other nineteenth century fringe groups, Mary Baker Eddy used trinitarian language to mean something different from mainstream Christians. The mainstream doctrine of the Trinity states that there is only one God, yet within the unity of the Godhead there are three divine Persons, Father, Son, and Holy Spirit, the three Persons being co-equal and co-eternal. Eddy summarized her view as follows: 'God the Father-Mother; Christ the spiritual idea of sonship; divine science or the Holy Comforter'.[36] 'Life, Truth, and Love constitute the triune Person called God, – that is, the triply divine Principle, Love. They represent a trinity in unity, three in one, – the same in essence, though multiform in office: God the Father-Mother; Christ the spiritual idea of sonship; divine Science or the Holy Comforter'.[37]

One of her followers explains, 'Mrs Eddy's concept of God, based on her long and faithful study of the Scriptures, was so exalted that she could not accept the divided authority which she felt to be implied in the orthodox doctrine of the Trinity, with its assumption of three persons in one God-head'.[38] Leaving aside that author's laudatory approach to Mary Baker Eddy, common to all Christian Science writers, it is clear that, despite what he says about 'her faithful study of the Scriptures', her change from biblical language indicated something more fundamental – a clear departure from the Bible's teaching concerning Christ and the Spirit. In particular, her interpretation of the Holy Spirit as divine Science (that is, Christian Science) paid scant regard to what the New Testament teaches of the Holy Spirit's personal being.

JESUS CHRIST

A Christian Scientist has written, 'I look especially to Jesus Christ as the Son of God and the Saviour of the world, whose life and healing ministry, redeeming the sinner, restoring the sick, and bringing joy to human existence, has opened up a radically different way of living'.[39] That contemporary testimony suggests that there are no great differences between Christian Science and mainstream Christian beliefs about Jesus Christ. Yet this is misleading, for behind the common terminology lie a number of fundamental differences.

Eddy described Christ as 'the spiritual idea of sonship'.[40] Two headings on page 473 of *Science and Health*, 'Christ the ideal Truth' and 'Jesus not God', provide a clear indication of the way Eddy's mind worked as she gave a fuller explanation of her doctrine of the Person of Jesus Christ.

Distinguishing between the human Jesus and the spiritual Christ idea,[41] Eddy believed in a duality of Jesus Christ.[42] Jesus was subject to human limitations but the Christ was 'without beginning of years or end of days'.[43] Whereas 'the corporeal man Jesus was human', the eternal Christ was 'incorporeal, spiritual, – yea, the divine image and likeness, dispelling the illusions of the senses'.[44] We should not confuse Jesus and the Christ, she argued. Instead, we should regard Jesus as the man who demonstrated the spiritual Christ, who expressed the highest type of divinity, which a fleshly form could express in that age. Jesus showed that 'Christ is the divine idea of God – the Holy Ghost, or Comforter, revealing the divine Principle, Love, and leading into all truth'.[45] Such beliefs led to Eddy's preferred title for Jesus, that of way-shower. His struggles in Gethsemane and Calvary 'enabled him to be the mediator, or way-shower, between God and men'.[46] Eddy also rejected Jesus Christ's deity, claiming that despite Jesus' embodiment and demonstration of God's truth, he was not God but the one who more than all others 'presented Christ, the true idea of God'.[47]

Pushed to its logical conclusion, therefore, Christian Science belief about Jesus Christ is belief in a real but impersonal *Christ Spirit* separated from an illusory *human Jesus*. This is in marked contrast to the New Testament, which states that the eternal Son of God came into the world to take up the position of the Christ. The Hebrew 'Messiah' and its Greek equivalent 'Christ', mean 'anointed', the recognized title of David's descendent who would one day come as Saviour. Peter proclaimed his belief that Jesus was this long-promised deliverer when he confessed, 'You are the Messiah, the Son of the living God'.[48] Eddy's idea of an eternal 'Christ spirit' has no place in the New Testament. It is also significant that Eddy identified the 'Christ', the Holy Spirit, and the Word, whereas mainstream Christians believe that Christ is a title given to Jesus, the incarnate Word, the second Person of the Trinity, that the Holy Spirit is the third Person of the Trinity, and that with the Father they are co-equal and co-eternal, for they are God. John 1 speaks of the eternal Word becoming flesh when Jesus was born of Mary, an important reminder that Jesus Christ, the incarnate Word, is both fully God and fully Man.

The New Testament test for an authentic view of Christ's Person remains 1 John 4.1–3: 'Test the spirits, to see whether they are from God; for there are many false prophets about in the world. The way to recognize the Spirit of God is this: every spirit which acknowledges that Jesus Christ **has come in the flesh** is from God'. Unlike Christian Scientists, John does not distinguish between Jesus and Christ. Morever, he points to the reality of Christ's material (in flesh) existence. On both these counts the Christian Science view of Christ fails the New Testament test.

MORTAL MIND

'Mortal mind' was Mary Baker Eddy's description of what she considered to be humanity's basic flaw. Because of 'mortal mind', men and women erroneously thought that God made the material creation, that they themselves had physical bodies made of material substance, and that sin and sickness were real. She claimed that matter was nothing more than 'a human concept', the product of 'mortal mind' which itself was under the delusion that the material universe, and human sin and sickness were real.[49]

Eddy defined 'mortal mind' as 'the flesh opposed to Spirit, the human mind and evil in contradistinction to the divine Mind, or Truth and good'.[50] She explained further that matter was another name for mortal mind and that 'mortal mind' was 'nothing claiming to be something'. Because true Mind (that is Spirit, God, Truth, Principle) was immortal, to speak of '*mortal* mind' was a contradiction.[51] 'Mortal mind' was nothing, it did not really exist, but it led to some erroneous beliefs, including the belief that the material world and its sin and sickness were real and that life itself had a beginning and an end.[52]

Despite what Eddy taught about its non-existence, 'mortal mind' played a vital role in her philosophy and had, and still has, significant repercussions for Christian Science belief and practice. In particular, it led to the denial of the reality sin and sickness. 'The only reality of sin, sickness, or death', Eddy stated, 'is the awful fact that unrealities seem real to human, erring belief, until God strips off their disguises'.[53] As we have seen, contemporary Christian Scientists explain that for them 'unreal' and 'real' do not mean what they mean for people outside their movement. Because 'real' relates only to what is *divinely* true, Christian Scientists say they are not claiming that sin and sickness are unreal in a *human* sense. However that may be, and the argument can be maintained only be ignoring or spiritualising much of the Bible, the fact remains that Eddy actually treated sin and sickness as if their only reality was in the unenlightened mortal minds of those who knew no better, and Christian Scientists do the same today.

SIN AND SALVATION

Eddy affirmed that because real humanity was spiritual, and therefore of God and good, spiritual humanity was without sin. Man was 'incapable of sin ... The real man cannot depart from holiness'.[54] Therefore, 'All that we term sin [is] a mortal belief'[55] and is nothing more than an 'error'.[56] The Christian Science way of salvation was then made clear. 'To get rid of sin through Science, is to divest sin of any supposed mind or reality ... You conquer error by denying its reality'.[57] We must deem it 'as devoid of reality'.[58] Eddy then reinterpreted the Bible to fit in with her philosophy and rewrote traditional Christian theology accordingly.

Rejecting the traditional Christian interpretation of the Fall, Eddy maintained that Genesis 3 should not be used to sustain the reality of either the material world or sin. 'Whatever indicates the fall of man or the opposite of God or God's absence is the Adam-dream, which is neither Mind nor man, for it is not begotten of the Father'.[59] Moreover, 'Sin exists here or hereafter only as long as the illusion of mind in matter remains. It is a sense of sin, and not a sinful soul, which is lost'.[60] Genesis 3 pointed to false belief about the reality of both matter and sin. To be saved from such non-existent sin required a transformation in human thinking.

Eddy then set about rewriting the Bible to square with such teaching. The biblical injunction to lay aside every weight, and the sin which so easily besets us[61] became, 'Let us put aside material self and sense and seek the divine Principle and Science of all healing'.[62] Isaiah 53.4–6, traditionally interpreted as pointing to the Lord's servant who would come to bear people's sins, became, 'Jesus bore our infirmities; he knew the error of mortal belief, and "with his stripes (the rejection of error) we are healed"'.[63] In an assertion which included words which to many mainstream Christians remain both offensive and heretical, she wrote, 'Jesus bore our sins in his body. He knew the mortal errors which constitute the material body, and could destroy those errors; but at the time when Jesus felt our infirmities, he had not conquered all the beliefs of the flesh or his sense of material life, nor had he risen to his final demonstration of spiritual power'.[64] The implication is clear. Jesus eventually became the person who best embodied Truth, but at this stage in his life he mistakenly believed in both sin and the reality of the material world. In time, however, he turned his back on such errors and afterwards could be described as the Christ who came 'to destroy *the belief of sin*'.[65]

Eddy had no time for the traditional Christian view that on the cross Jesus was suffering vicariously for the sins of the world. She described Christ's role in atonement as that of the 'way-shower', which was her rendering of the biblical world 'mediator'. More careful attention to the context of 'mediator' in 1 Timothy would have shown her the insufficiency of 'way shower' as a translation. The writer states, 'There is one God, and there is one mediator between God and man, the man Christ Jesus, who gave himself as a ransom for all'.[66] A 'mediator' is an arbitrator or peacemaker who acts to remove a disagreement between two parties, and a 'ransom' is a price paid for release. By bringing these two powerful words together to describe the work of Jesus Christ for our salvation, the writer is stressing the price the Son of God paid to set us free from sin and to bring us back into a right relationship with God.

This theme, essential to an understanding of New Testament teaching, found no place in Eddy's theology. She provided a whole chapter in *Science and Health* to correct it, demonstrating in the process how little she understood the mainstream Christian view, despite her traditional Christian upbringing. Final deliverance from error was not achieved, she maintained, by 'pinning one's faith without works to another's vicarious effort' and those who believed that divinity was appeased by human suffering, did not understand God.[67] Admitting that the atonement was 'a hard problem in theology', she stated that 'its scientific explanation', by which she meant her own Christian Science view, was that suffering was an error of sinful sense which Truth destroyed.[68] She pointed out that she differed from the view of 'erudite theology' which regarded the crucifixion 'as providing a ready pardon for all sinners who ask for it and are willing to be forgiven'.[69] Instead, 'The efficacy of the crucifixion lay in the practical affection and goodness it demonstrated for mankind'.[70] 'The material blood of Jesus was no more efficacious to cleanse from sin when it was shed upon "the accursed tree", than when it was flowing in his veins'.[71]

Leaving aside the crude and insensitive way she attempted to demolish the traditional view of the atonement, it is clear that the traditional Christian view is very different. It is based on three main strands in the Bible's teaching about humanity. First, because we are made in God's image, we all have great potential for good. Secondly, despite the fact that we are made in God's image, we are all flawed by sin: in all of us the image of God is defaced, though not obliterated. Thirdly, through Christ, who is God's answer to human sin and in whom we see God's image in its perfection, we can be forgiven, restored to a right relationship with God, the image of God can be renewed, and our human potential can be realized. In short, the mainstream Christian view of humanity:

- is not completely pessimistic – we are not as bad as we might be;
- is not entirely optimistic – we are not necessarily becoming better as we grow older;
- is totally realistic – though both our problem and our potential are great, in Christ we can begin to become what God has always intended us to be. That process starts in this life and will be completed in eternity.

Mainstream Christians acknowledge with Paul and the New Testament generally that this material world is *transitory*: it will not last forever. They also believe, however, that this is a real physical world in which sin, sickness and death are all too dreadfully present. At the same time they see that the Bible holds out the hope of a future in which there will be no more sin, suffering, and death. They therefore take at its face value the clear scriptural teaching that it was to this present, material world that God sent his Son as its Saviour. Christ offered himself on the cross as solution to mankind's basic problem. By sacrificing himself for the sin of the world, the incarnate Son of God acted to bring people back into that fellowship with God which they had forfeited through sin. This is all summed up in traditional Christian theology with words like 'atonement', 'salvation' and 'wholeness'.

Mainstream Christians believe that they are saved, therefore, not through any merits of their own, but by God's grace, his free, unmerited favour and goodness held out to them in the Son of God, who loved them and gave himself up for them. They believe also that they begin to receive all that God offers them (that is, they begin to become whole) as they respond through faith, trusting Christ as Saviour and acknowledging him as Lord.[72] Mainstream Christians further believe that by dying on humanity's behalf, Jesus Christ bridged the gap between God and ourselves caused by our sinfulness, and so through Christ's atonement we are brought into a right relationship with God, we are at one with him.

HEALING

As we have seen, the Christian Science attitude to both sin and disease arises directly out of the assertion that neither has any reality beyond that of the false reality given to it by the person who believes it exists. It is an error of mortal mind. Eddy went so far as to claim that 'a physical diagnosis of disease – since mortal mind must be the cause of disease – tends to induce disease'.[73]

Christian Science practitioners, the movement's trained and authorized healers, make no attempt to address the illness itself. Instead, following the basic philosophy of the unreality of physical illness, they try to focus the thoughts of the sick person on that perfect Mind or Principle which is God. Eddy prescribed this healing method. 'Turn their thoughts away from their bodies to higher objects. Teach them that their being is sustained by Spirit, not by matter, and that they find health, peace, and harmony in God, divine Love'.[74] Dewitt John explains further: 'A patient with a physical problem visiting a Christian Science practitioner may be surprised to find that the practitioner will make little or no inquiry about symptoms, and will, in fact, avoid any detailed discussion of them, turning the patient's thought away from the body to a discussion of the nature of God and man in His likeness'.[75]

Christian Scientists do not normally use ordinary medical practitioners. They believe that normal medical practice and Christian Science practice 'are so vastly different in diagnostic approach, in their concept of the nature of disease, and in their healing procedure, that they cannot work in co-operation' and any attempt to do so 'would be unfair to both systems and dangerous to the patient'.[76] What Dewitt John calls 'the

Christian Science concept of the nature of disease' is that all disease is essentially a mental condition, and that 'sick thoughts make sick bodies'.[77] Health problems which appear to consist of physical conditions are seen as 'wholly a mental problem'.[78] The aim of Christian Science is, therefore 'to wipe out the mental elements which produce sickness and discord'.[79] A recent Christian Science publication underlines this basic approach 'Sickness is one expression of the fundamental error of the mortal mind that accepts existence as something separate from God'.[80]

Despite their belief in the unreality of sickness, however, members of the movement often appear to be inconsistent. Eddy herself wore glasses and dentures, and received morphine injections to relieve pain from a stone in the kidney. She justified this as follows: 'If from an injury or from any cause, a Christian Scientist were seized with pain so violent that he could not treat himself mentally – and the Scientists had failed to relieve him – the sufferer could call a surgeon, who would give him a hypodermic injection; then, when the belief of pain was lulled, he could handle his own case mentally. Thus it is that we 'prove all things; (and) hold fast that which is good'.[81] She advised, 'Until the advancing age admits the efficacy and supremacy of Mind, it is better for Christian Scientists to leave surgery and the adjustment of broken bones and dislocations to the fingers of a surgeon, while the mental healer confines himself chiefly to mental reconstruction and to the prevention of inflammation'.[82]

Christian Scientists are not the only religious believers whose practice does not always match their profession, so it ill behoves the rest of us to be over-critical in this area. It does raise question marks, however, about how firm they are in their basic conviction that, when people appear to be sick, the alleged reality of their physical condition is merely a delusion of their unregenerate mortal minds.

There is at least one practical refutation of these ideas about mortal mind and illness. If someone eats or drinks something poisonous, believing in his mortal mind that it is innocuous, the poison may still kill him. Eddy's ingenious explanation reads as follows: 'In such cases a few persons believe the potion swallowed by the patient to be harmless, but the vast majority of mankind, though they know nothing of this particular case and this special person, believe the arsenic, the strychnine, or what-ever the drug used, to be poisonous, for it is set down as a poison by mortal mind. Consequently, the result is controlled by the majority of opinions, not by the infinitesimal minority of opinions in the sick-chamber'.[83] It seems to have escaped Eddy's thought that the argument she puts forward would also rule out the possibility of all Christian

Science healings on the grounds that almost everyone apart from Christian Scientists believe in the reality of the sickness.

Without doubt a number of people have become practising Christian Scientists through their experience of healing. The movement claims that some of those considered 'beyond hope because of physical maladies' decide to 'try Christian Science' as a last resort and that large numbers 'have been restored, entirely by spiritual means'. Christian Science denies the charge that its cures are almost all of a psychosomatic nature, claiming healings of cancer, arthritis, and other organic conditions, sometimes far advanced.[84] Every Wednesday evening Christian Scientists share stories of such healings, and there is no doubt that cures do take place, but it is difficult to test the nature of such cures when the only evidence offered is anecdotal.

The movement claims that these testimonies of healing demonstrate the truth of Christian Science beliefs, but it is important to be clear that, even when healing does occur, this is not in itself proof of the reliability of the belief system on which cures are said to be based. Mainstream Christians, Spiritualists, New Age followers, and many others can also point to some evidence of healing brought about through their churches or movements, and it is clear that the belief systems behind all of these differ fundamentally. They cannot all be true. Whatever else we may say about healing, therefore, it cannot be used as evidence of the authenticity of the teaching of the movement sponsoring the healers.

A mainstream Christian approach to healing starts from a belief in the reality, though also in the impermanence, of physical and mental disorders. Mainstream Christians also believe that all human beings are subject to the consequences of being part of a fallen humanity, which by and large has turned its back on God. Sickness and suffering are among the consequences that inevitably follow. Christians are no more immune to sickness and suffering than are other human beings.

Human beings are a complicated and indivisable combination of body-mind-spirit, not simply physical bodies, or mere packages of mental energy, or ethereal spirits. Because of this essential unity, illness is seldom (if ever) simply physical, or mental, or spiritual, and the same can be said of healing. We should all be grateful to God when healing comes, whether through normal medical channels, in direct answer to prayer, or as if often the case a combination of the two. When healing does not come, however, we can find strength to cope with it through the knowledge that the God, who himself experienced suffering in his incarnate Son, is with us in our suffering. Like Paul, we are to look to God for his strength to be made perfect in weakness. Though rejecting Mary Baker Eddy's belief system, therefore, we can agree with Christian Scientists, medical practitioners, and many others, that a positive mental and spiritual attitude towards sickness, including prayer, can be a strong contributory factor in recovery. But the view that sickness exists only in an unregenerate 'mortal mind' can be a very dangerous path to follow.

POSTSCRIPT

This chapter has dealt almost entirely with the beliefs of Mary Baker Eddy, the Christian Science founder. Most of the references are direct quotations from her textbook, *Science and Health with Key to the Scriptures*. Other authors have been used only where they throw light on Eddy's beliefs,. In view of this, it is perhaps necessary in concluding this examination of Christian Science to re-emphasise what was stated at its outset. The belief system of this movement is that set out by Mary Baker Eddy. The interpretation of the Bible accepted in the movement today is exactly the same as that expounded in Eddy's textbook, *Science and Health with Key to the Scriptures*. There have been no changes, and nor can there be; for Eddy ensured by legal means that her followers must accept without question and for ever what she has written in the Christian Science textbook.

WHERE CHRISTIAN SCIENTISTS AND MAINSTREAM CHRISTIANS PART COMPANY

CHRISTIAN SCIENTISTS	MAINSTREAM CHRISTIANS
The Bible	
Although the Bible is God's inspired Word and is a sufficient guide to eternal life, it needs the inspired interpretation provided by Mary Baker Eddy's *Science and Health with Key to the Scriptures* if it is to be properly understood. Her book is the Church's textbook which alone reveals the spiritual truths in that other revelation, the Bible.	God has revealed all that he wants us to know of himself and his will for us in Christ, his incarnate Word and what we know of Christ is contained in the Bible, his written word. The Bible is the norm by which all claims to religious truth are to be measured, including those claiming inspiration in interpreting the scriptures.

CHRISTIAN SCIENTISTS	MAINSTREAM CHRISTIANS

God

God, Spirit, Truth, Love, Principle is All-in-all, the Creator of the spiritual (not material) creation, the only reality beside which there is no other might or Mind. God is a tri-unity: Father-Mother; Christ, the spiritual idea of sonship; and divine science or the Holy Comforter.	God is Father, Son and Holy Spirit, three Persons within the unity of the Godhead. God is Creator of all that is, including the impermanent material world and all who inhabit it.

Jesus Christ

Jesus Christ is a duality: Christ is the spiritual Truth; Jesus is not God but the man who more than all others embodied and demonstrated the Christ idea. Jesus Christ is the way-shower, not the vicarious sufferer who died to take away our sins. The cross was a demonstration of practical affection and goodness. The blood of Jesus is not efficacious to cleanse from sin.	Jesus Christ is the eternal Son of the Father. He became incarnate, taking up our humanity into his Godhood, for our salvation. In his unique Person, the divine and the human natures are united. He is the one mediator between God and man, and gave himself as a ransom for all. Through that sacrificial death on the Cross we may be brought back into a right relationship with God from whom, without Christ, we are separated by our sin.

CHRISTIAN SCIENTISTS	MAINSTREAM CHRISTIANS

Salvation

The material world and material humanity with its sin, suffering and death, are unreal, an illusion of mortal mind. Real humanity is spiritual, of God and therefore good and without sin. Jesus Christ is the way-shower, demonstrating that salvation or wholeness comes as we conquer the error of sin as, like him, we deny its reality.

Achieved by Christ, who died on the cross and rose again for us, salvation is not something we earn by obedience or in any other way, but is God's gracious gift which is appropriated through trusting in Christ as Saviour. The same full salvation, or wholeness, is offered to all in Christ. It does not depend upon our level of obedience: we obey God, not to achieve salvation, but because we love him for what he has done for us in Christ.

The Church

Whereas the Churches of mainstream Christianity have largely lost their way because they have misunderstood the Bible's message, through the writings of its founder Christian Science has rediscovered the truth. The Mother Church in Boston and its branches throughout the world are a reinstatement of original Christianity and its lost element of healing. Christian Science has no ordained clergy: all its lay members are encouraged to participate fully; some are appointed to specific roles.

The one true Church is that founded on the apostles and prophets, with Christ as the chief cornerstone. It consists of all who have accepted Christ as Saviour and acknowledge him as Lord. The whole Church is a holy priesthood, though within its membership some are called (and often ordained) to specific roles of leadership.

REFERENCES

1. *Miscellaneous Writings*, page 24.
2. Encyclopaedia Britannica, 1984.
3. Dewitt John, *The Christian Science Way of Life*, page 148.
4. Mary Baker Eddy, *Science and Health with Key to the Scriptures*, page 108.
5. Dewitt John op. cit. page 27.
6. ibid, page 39.
7. *Science and Health*, page 497.
8. T.L. Leishmann, *Why I am a Christian Scientist*.
9. Mary Baker Eddy, *Miscellany*, pages 114f.
10. Mary Baker Eddy, *Church Manual*, page 17.
11. Bryan Wilson, *Sects and Society*, pages 149ff.
12. ibid, page 156.
13. ibid, page 212.
14. ibid.
15. Dewitt John, op. cit., page 17.
16. Stephen Gottschalk, article, *Encylopaedia of Religion*.
17. Dewitt John, op. cit., page 68.
18. *Science and Health*, pages 472f.
19. *Christian Science: A Source of Contemporary Materials*, page 298.
20. ibid, page 9.
21. 2 Corinthians 4.18.
22. 2 Corinthians 5.1.
23. *Science and Health*, page 275.
24. *Science and Health*, page 531.
25. *Science and Health*, page 502.
26. *Science and Health*, page 510.
27. *Science and Health*, page 511.
28. *Science and Health*, page 516.
29. *Science and Health*, page 522.
30. *Christian Science: A Sourcebook of Contemporary Materials*, page 88.
31. Colin Brown, *Philosophy and the Christian Faith*, pages 53–56.
32. Stephen Gottschalk, article, *The Encyclopaedia of Religion*.
33. *Science and Health*, page 332.
34. *Science and Health*, page 587.
35. *Science and Health*, page 116.
36. *Science and Health*, page 331.
37. *Science and Health*, page 331.
38. Leishmann, op. cit.
39. Christian Science: *A Sourcebook of Contemporary Materials*, page 31.
40. *Science and Health*, page 331.
41. *Science and Health*, page 332.
42. *Science and Health*, page 473.
43. *Science and Health*, page 333.
44. *Science and Health*, page 332.
45. *Science and Health*, page 332.
46. *Science and Health*, page 30.
47. *Science and Health*, page 473.
48. Matthew 16.16.
49. *Science and Health*, page 469.
50. *Science and Health*, page 50.
51. *Science and Health*, page 591.

52. *Science and Health*, page 592.
53. *Science and Health*, page 472.
54. *Science and Health*, page 475.
55. *Science and Health*, page 278.
56. *Science and Health*, page 473.
57. *Science and Health*, page 339.
58. *Science and Health*, page 525.
59. *Science and Health*, page 282.
60. *Science and Health*, page 311.
61. Hebrews 12.1.
62. *Science and Health*, page 20.
63. *Science and Health*, page 20.
64. *Science and Health*, page 53.
65. *Science and Health*, page 473.
66. I Timothy 2.5f. RSV.
67. *Science and Health*, page 22.
68. *Science and Health*, page 23.
69. *Science and Health*, page 24.
70. *Science and Health*, page 24.
71. *Science and Health*, page 25.
72. Ephesians 2.8, Galatians 2.20.
73. *Science and Health*, page 370.
74. *Science and Health*, page 416.
75. Dewitt John, op. cit., page 153.
76. ibid, page 18.
77. ibid, page 26.
78. ibid, page 121.
79. ibid, page 129.
80. *Christian Science: A Sourcebook of Contemporary Materials*, page 8.
81. *Science and Health*, page 464.
82. *Science and Health*, page 401.
83. *Science and Health*, pages 171f.
84. Dewitt John, op. cit., pages 12f.

Chapter 7

NEW AGE

Putting together jigsaw puzzles has never been one of my favourite past-times. I lack the patience. I do not easily recognise which piece fits in where. And I always have the sneaking suspicion that I shall come to the end only to find that an important piece of the jigsaw is missing. I have to confess similar feelings as I write about New Age. If New Age were a jigsaw puzzle, there would be the further complication that some of the pieces do not fit because they seem to come from a different puzzle! To change the metaphor, trying to grasp what is meant by New Age is like trying to grab hold of a piece of soap in the bath.

WHAT IS 'NEW AGE'? – Towards a definition

New Age can be described variously as a capacious umbrella sheltering many different and sometimes contradictory ideas, a collection of beliefs and practices from a variety of sources, an all-inclusive, syncretistic movement tolerant of almost anything, and, less flatteringly, a ragbag of philosophical, religious, psychological and scientific ideas, and a 'pick-and-mix' religion. For many people New Age is a response to their deeply felt spiritual needs without the shackles (as they see them) of mainstream Christianity. One adherent has written, 'I see the New Age phenomenon as the visible tip of an iceberg of a mass movement in which humanity is reasserting its right to explore spirituality in total freedom. The constraints of religious and intellectual ideology are falling away'.[1]

The significance of that comment lies in the clause, 'to explore spirituality in total freedom'. That is why New Age is so difficult to define, for one person's freedom leads him one way, another's leads her in a different direction. That is also why New Age is different from, and to some extent opposed to, mainstream Christianity. The Christian view that God reveals himself (and therefore his truth) uniquely in his incarnate Word, Jesus Christ, and through his written word, the Bible, is seen as too restricting for those wishing to make their own undirected tour of spirituality.

One of the problems facing anyone writing about the New Age Movement is the choice of what to include and what to leave out. As Eileen Barker points out, 'The New Age "label" has been applied relatively indiscriminately both by those for whom it is a proud affirmation and by those for whom it is a term of abuse.' She suggests that some commentators would include those involved in various branches of the Human Potential movement, Occultism, Neo-Paganism, Witchcraft, Shamanism and even Satanism.[2] In fact, because the term 'New Age' has been used so indiscriminately and also because some greedy people have cashed in on some of the fads associated with it to make a lot of money, some New Agers are arguing for a change of name. Among the suggested alternatives is the less-than-snappy name, 'New Era of Awareness'.[3]

That problem is further compounded by the fact that New Age followers see it as all-embracing, encompassing all that is best in modern knowledge and ancient wisdom. So they try to integrate the new ideas of science, ecology and psychology with many of the ancient but neglected 'truths' of almost every religious tradition. A quick glance at the New Age shelves of any modern bookshop demonstrates the size of this problem.

One prominent British exponent of New Age thinking, Dr William Bloom, however, though acknowledging the diversity of the movement, sees it as possessing an underlying unity. Although it 'represents several different dynamics' they 'thread together to communicate the same message: there is an invisible and inner dimension to all life – cellular, human and cosmic'. For Bloom, 'To explore this inner reality' is 'the most exciting work in the world'.[4] At the heart of the New Age, then, is belief in the basic unity, the essential oneness, of all, which is character-istic of philosophical systems such as monism and pantheism and seen particularly in Hinduism. Although Bloom's words do not provide us with a comprehensive map of New Age thinking, they give us some significant clues to help us in our search for it.

Positively, New Agers claim that it is:

- the belief that there is an invisible and inner dimension to all life;
- an experiential and individual search for that inner reality;
- a totally free spiritual quest, necessitating the rejection of the crippling inhibitions and constraints of religious and intellectual ideologies.

Negatively, New Agers make clear that it is not:

- a clearly defined body of belief and practice to which all New Agers adhere;
- a single organisation to which all New Agers belong;
- the unquestioning following of a charismatic leader.

We shall need to return to some of these themes, for they indicate both the recurring ideas in New Age thinking and the reasons why New Agers regard mainstream Christianity with such suspicion. What is clear, however, is that 'fluidity' is a key-word when considering how the movement organises itself, what its members believe and practise, and to whom New Agers look for leadership. Getting to know the New Age Movement may sometimes feel like trying to nail jelly to the ceiling!

Despite such difficulties, New Age is not something which mainstream Christians can simply reject out of hand. Some of its ideas are shared with other people who would not wish to be labelled as New Age. So, for example, holistic medicine, feminism, vegetarianism and ecological concern are shared with many outside the New Age movement, including many mainstream Christians.

This, then, is the New Age movement. What makes it distinctive? Are there landmarks to guide us? Are there any boundaries? Or is it all open countryside over which any may roam freely, collecting what they will? And is it as *new* as it thinks?

In a recent comprehensive examination and critique of the movement, Michael Perry, Sub Dean of Durham Cathedral, has said that the movement's ideas 'like ecologically-friendly paper, are 100% re-cycled'.[5] He adds that New Agers see this as a positive virtue. The movement brings together various ways of looking at the world. 'We are not dealing with a monolithic organisation or with a single set of mutually consistent beliefs, but with a whole variety of ways of looking at the world towards the end of the second millennium.'[6] New Agers themselves admit that some of the beliefs and practices found within the movement make very strange bed-fellows, whilst the former Archbishop of Canterbury, Lord Runcie, described New Age as a mix of eclecticism, mysticism, and syncretism reacting against the materialistic scepticism of today's society.[7] Almost anyone and anything is welcome. Almost, but not quite, for as we have seen the movement is tolerant of almost anything except the unique and distinctive claims of Christianity, for these are seen as shackles constraining and in time crippling those who persist with them.

WHO ARE THE NEW AGE LEADERS?

Most of the religious movements considered in previous chapters can point to a founder, a charismatic leader, who gave the movement its initial impetus and upon whose work later leaders were able to build. In trying to understand New Age, however, we are dealing, not just with one influential founder, but with a number of personalities all of whom have contributed to the movement's development, and some of whom have set up their own 'New Age' centres.

Alice Bailey

A 'New Ager' before the movement really began, Alice Bailey was one of the most formative influences in its evolution. She was a theosophist who claimed to be acting as secretary of a dead Tibertan teacher, Dywhal Khul, and wrote a number of books claiming to set out his esoteric philosophy. Many consider them to be the key inspiration of the New Age Movement.[8] She certainly sowed some of the seeds of the thoroughgoing syncretistic approach to religion which is one of the movement's chief characteristics.

Alice Bailey wished to encourage the emergence of a universal religion, which she called 'the one Church'.[9] As such a religion emerged, she believed, theologies would disappear into the knowledge of God; doctrines and dogmas would no longer be regarded as necessary, for faith would be based on experience, and authority would give place to personal appreciation of Reality. She claimed that in the meantime we were passing through a period of chaos and questioning in which traditional religious belief was being challenged by scientific and historical research and established ideas about God, the soul, man and destiny were being rejected.

Alice Bailey argued that two main lines of thought were emerging out of the medley of ideas, theories, speculations, religions, churches, cults, sects and organisations. On the one hand were those who looked back to the past, clinging to old theologies and authorities such as the Bible and the prophet. They were doomed eventually to die out. On the other hand were the 'inner group of lovers of God, the intellectual mystics, the knowers of reality who belong to no one religion or organisation, but who regard themselves as members of the Church universal'. They would strengthen and grow until they gave birth to the ultimate formulation of truth.[10] Within such a scheme, Alice Bailey saw no place for a unique world saviour such as those of the passing world religions. They were being superseded by a kind of 'group Saviour' or 'group Avatar'. Because this emerging 'group Saviour' was made up of 'knowers of God', it would build the New Age.[11]

Marilyn Ferguson

Although Alice Bailey ideas undoubtedly helped to provide an environment in which New Age thinking could develop, it is Marilyn Ferguson's influence from the early 1980s onwards which has given the movement particular impetus. Her book *The Aquarian Conspiracy*, first published in 1981 but reprinted a number of times since, is regarded by many as an essential introduction to the New Age phenomenon.

Arguing from an astrological base, she says we are passing from the so-called Age of Pisces, the Fish, into the New Age of Aquarius, the Water Carrier. The Age of Pisces, covering the period from the beginning of Christianity until the present, is seen as the age of authority, with every-thing conceived in black and white terms. During this period Christianity and Judaism have dominated all the thinking in the western world. The New Age of Aquarius introduces much more fluidity into thought and action and thus breaks the crippling hold of Christianity.

To come to terms with this New Age of Aquarius, we require what Ferguson calls a 'paradigm shift', 'a distinctly new way of thinking about old problems'. It is like the new way of looking at things which resulted from the impact of Einstein's theory of relativity, when Newton's mechanistic physics was superseded. 'Our understanding of nature shifted from a clockwork paradigm to an uncertainty paradigm, from the absolute to the relative'.[12] Such a fundamental 'paradigm shift' is now required to meet the challenge of the emerging Age of Aquarius. We can, of course, choose to cling to the old, or we can choose to welcome the new. If we cling to the old, continuing to believe in a world of fixity, we shall fight change. If, on the other hand, we choose the new, believing instead in a world of fluidity, we shall welcome and co-operate with change.[13] Ferguson's New Age philosophy therefore challenges us to allow our minds to be transformed. Such a trans-formation will result in a move from the competitive to the collaborative and will affect medicine, business, marriage, leisure, scientific research – everything.

Ferguson makes much of modern research about the right and left hemispheres of the brain. The brain's left hemisphere is generally concerned with logical and rational thinking and is analytical, whilst the right hemisphere is intuitive and concerned with wholeness. Her new way of looking at reality – the paradigm shift – is a shift from the mechanistic to the holistic, from a left-brain approach to life to a right brain approach. She believes that too many people use only half their brains. 'Cut off from the fantasy, dreams, intuitions, and holistic processes of the right brain, the left is sterile. And the right brain, cut off from integration with its organising partner, keeps recycling its emotional charge. Feelings are dammed, perhaps to work private mischief in fatigue, illness, neuroses.' Such fragmentation costs us 'our health and our capacity for intimacy', as well as 'our ability to learn, create, innovate'.[14]

This is all very interesting, if a little heady, but where is it leading? What is the aim of those accepting and applying Marilyn Ferguson's philosophy? She explains that what she calls her Aquarian conspirators are a leaderless but powerful network working to bring about radical change. They have 'broken with certain key elements of Western thought, and they may even have broken continuity with history'. They are working for 'the turnabout in consciousness of a critical number of individuals, enough to bring about a renewal of society'.[15] Before this can happen, however, these workers for radical change themselves need to be changed. So Marilyn Ferguson stresses the need for individual transformation, involving among other things the development of the individual's potential to the full.

Shirley MacLaine

Whereas Marilyn Ferguson's main contribution to the New Age has been to provide an intellectual framework within which its members work, Shirley MacLaine, the American media personality, has given New Age a tremendous boost through her TV programmes and books. In her autobiography, *Out on a Limb*, she describes her traditional Christian upbringing in an American Baptist home, where belief in God and regular churchgoing were taken for granted. As a teenager she began to question traditional Christian beliefs but still clung to the view that the spiritual and supernatural dimensions of religion were the things that made sense of life. She explored other religions as she travelled the world until eventually she was persuaded that she was being told that her spiritual needs could be met if she immersed herself in the warm mineral waters at the top of the Andes. Following Naaman of old, she did as she was told and, she claimed, the combined effect of the warm water, the aroma and deep breathing exercises gave her the first of many out-of-body experiences in which she believed she rose into some higher order of existence. She later described this experience (which was to be followed by many others) as 'astral projection' and 'rebirth'. It is not uncommon for many who have followed the Shirley MacLaine way to practise such immersions once a week and like her to find renewal through them. Many other New Agers focus on the breathing exercises rather than on the immersions.

George Trevelyan

Starting in California and spreading quickly through the influence of such leaders and some significant blockbuster films like ET and Superman which popularised New Age ideas, the movement has made a tremendous impact in the United States. Though not so strong in the United Kingdom, it probably attracts more followers than all the religious sects and cults put together. Its United Kingdom growth owes much to Sir George Trevelyan, whom New Agers themselves regard as 'the father-figure of the New Age movement in Britain'.[16] Michael Perry says Trevelyan 'has been more influential (probably) than any other single person in the UK in the promulgation of New Age ideas'.[17]

Trevelyan emphasises a number of things including:
* the sacredness of all life;
* the need for daily meditation as a 'ritual of inner listening which leads to a blending with the Creative Intelligence';
* organically grown food and vegetarianism;
* belief in 'invisible planes of consciousness interweaving with our material world', peopled by those we love but have died and with whom we have telepathic contact;
* the conviction that our lives on earth (of which there will be many for each individual) are training schools for souls, equipping people to see what life on earth is really about;
* and the view that death means release from the limitations of materiality.

Of particular interest to Christians is Trevelyan's view that the 'Christ', the principle of love, is not to be identified with Jesus in the way that it has been by Christians. He believes that the 'Christos' entered Jesus at his baptism and for three years inhabited that body. He interprets the Second Coming as each person having the same experience, the en-Christing of us all.

David Spangler

Another important British influence in the New Age movement is that of David Spangler of the Findhorn Foundation operating from the Foundation's community at Findhorn Bay on the Moray Firth, Scotland. The community has attracted much media attention because of the enormous size of its vegetables. Members claim that this all started when Dorothy Maclean, one of three people working on a garden project there in the 1960s, contacted nature spirits through Channelling. The spirits told her that the success of the project depended on the group co-operating with the spirits. When they responded positively to this advice, their project prospered beyond their wildest dreams.

Spangler joined the group some years later and had a hand in the founding of the Findhorn Trust and the later Findhorn Foundation, and has made a significant impact there and throughout the New Age movement ever since. The community, which has become an important resource centre for New Age in Britain, producing New Age publications and running its own educational programme, has attracted about 150 members from a number of countries. According to Stephanie Cole, 'It's a sort of experiment in community living, with a tremendous spiritual bias. It's very eclectic, very broad based. The bias is towards Christianity, but it encompasses all belief systems'.[18] One of its main emphases is the basic New Age monistic philosophy, the one-ness of all, and it seeks to encourage people to recognise the unity which they have with the whole of creation.

William Bloom

Another important New Age teacher in the United Kingdom is Dr William Bloom, a psychology teacher at the London School of Economics. Dr Bloom is founding director of the New Age programme, 'Alternatives', at St James' Church, Piccadilly, London and is also closely associated with Spangler and the Findhorn Foundation. He was one of those responsible for the 1991 Channel Four television programme on the New Age Movement and edited the Channel Four book, *The New Age – An Anthology of Essential Writings*.

According to Bloom, the New Age Movement is concerned with what he calls four major fields: new science; ecology; new psychology; and spiritual dynamics.

Beginning with the new science, Bloom refers to 'all the new theories which are reworking our intellectual understanding of the structures of life', notably the new insights of sub-atomic physics, cosmology and biology. He points out that Newton's mechanistic view of the cosmos – tangible bits and pieces following reliable laws of interaction – has given way to a more fluid and expanded view of reality. A consequence is that matter and energy are seen as bound together in invisible ways; that matter, energy and consciousness are one continuum: and this means that 'All life is intimately connected'.[19]

Bloom says that this 'new science' supports a new understanding of the earth as a complete living organism and of New Age views about ecology. 'The concept of interdependence and interpenetration across all species expands to include not only our actions as consumers and workers but also the total energy effect of our actions and attitudes.' [20]

Moving on to psychology, Bloom says that the new psychology demonstrates not only the repressed and primitive areas of the unconscious – as in Freud – but also the extraordinary dynamics of the supraconscious and transpersonal. From this comes his conviction that 'all people are capable of becoming integrated, fulfilled and completely loving human beings'.[21]

Bloom then moves into his fourth field, the power of spiritual dynamics, which he calls the 'the hallmark of the New Age'. It would seem that the power lies in the fact that New Age spirituality draws its lessons and inspirations from many sources and brings them together. So, rubbing shoulders with each other, we find elements of Gnosticism, Judaism, Islam and Buddhism, together with Wicca and Druidism and the traditions of North American Indians, Australian Aborigines, and African medicine people.

It is clear, therefore, that the growing interest in, and support for, New Age owes much to these and other influential teachers. Some of them have endeavoured to show that New Age thought is intellectually respectable. Others, notably Shirley MacLaine, have given the movement a high profile through the wide appeal of the media. All have struck a chord with thousands who, though finding little attraction in the more traditional expressions of religion, nevertheless believe that they have spiritual needs which a materialistic society has failed to satisfy. The mainstream Churches need to ask why such spiritually hungry people have turned to *The New Age* groups, rather than to mainstream Christianity, to have their needs met.

Although New Age has no single charismatic founder, unlike the sects and cults examined earlier, these six people have all made significant contributions to New Age growth in the western world. It is from them, and a number of others like them, that the plethora of New Age beliefs and practices have sprung.

NEW AGE BELIEFS AND PRACTICES

An invisible spiritual dimension to all life

Earlier in this book religious sects were defined as movements of religious protest. Although New Age cannot be defined as a single sect, its followers, despite all their diversity in belief and practice, together make up a religious protest movement. The characteristic outworkings of the protest will vary from person to person and place to place, but the starting point is generally the same: disillusionment with, and rejection of, the materialistic outlook of western culture and a growing recognition that there is an invisible and inner dimension to all life. Along with this has gone the rejection of organised religion, represented in the United Kingdom largely by Christianity, and the desire to replace it with a 'New Age' spirituality.

Syncretism

If this basic subjectivism of the New Age is accepted, it follows that we shall have to give up thinking that the truth is to be found within any one religious organisation and instead adopt a syncretistic attitude – a kind of pick-and-mix religion – selecting whatever appeals in any of the religions or from primitive beliefs. Almost anything is permissible to New Age followers, it would seem, except the inhibiting views of mainstream Christianity and Judaism. New Agers are quite happy to bring into their system karma, reincarnation and astrology from Eastern Religions, together with aspects of Druidism and Witchcraft from paganism, other occult practices like the use of tarot cards and ouija boards, belief in the earth as the Mother Goddess Gaia from Greek mythology, and ideas about channelling which are very close to mediumship in Spiritualism.

Karma and Reincarnation

Stephanie Cole, one of the best known British television stars, explains how she turned from the Christianity of her childhood, explored humanism and various religious ideas including those of Buddhism, and then returned to Christianity through reading the psychologist, Carl Jung. She now finds help and encouragement in her spiritual pilgrimage at St James' Church, Piccadilly, a meeting place between Christians and New Age followers, and at the Findhorn community in Scotland. Like many attracted by New Age spirituality, she tries to blend her own Christianity with New Age philosophy and practice. 'My personal belief system', she explains, 'encompasses the idea of reincarnation.' [22]

Karma and reincarnation (or the transmigration of souls) were an integral part of the major world religions of the East thousands of years before the arrival of the New Age movement. In its simplest form, karma is the idea that every activity in a person's life, whether of thought or deed, leads to a series of consequences, just as a stone thrown into a pool of water results in an expanding series of ripples. When that person dies, there is this accumulation of karma, merit and demerit, to be worked out and this leads to a kind of chain reaction of what the person has been and has done and determines that person's status in the following existence. So, depending on his or her karma, a person may return as another person of a higher or lower status, as an animal, as a plant, or as something else. In its harshest form belief in karma can lead people to adopt an attitude of complete indifference to the suffering of their fellow human beings, because it is believed that the sufferer is working through his or her karma, is reaping what was sown in a previous existence. Only when the effects have been fully worked out is the person set free from the endless cycle of birth and rebirth to become completely absorbed in Ultimate Reality, like a drip of water being lost in a bucket full.

Western New Age followers interpret this Hindu philosophy more flexibly. Stephanie Cole, for example, explains: 'The soul has to be refined and refined until it can come back forever to that place from which it comes, that source of energy. So you keep being born until you have got it right'.[23] Like many New Agers, she believes that she has some control over what will happen in her next reincarnated life. 'I like the thought of my soul sitting up there and looking down thinking, "Okay, Kid, so what's the lesson this lifetime?" and "Okay, that's a good parent to choose if you want to learn that particular lesson".'[24]

Channelling

Though akin to spiritualism in that channelling is believed to be a means of contacting beings of another world, it is different from it in that it makes no claim to contact the departed spirits of living relatives. New Age channellers believe that they become channels or intermediaries for the extra-terrestrial inhabitants of a world usually invisible to our own, to spirit guides endowed with much greater wisdom than that which we possess. These beings, through whom we can be linked by those who from time to time in trance-like states embody them, provide very specific and detailed guidance on all the matters, great or small, which concern us – though usually at a price!

In the United States, where channelling has become big business, theatres are filled with seekers after such wisdom willing to pay quite high entrance fees to see such beings perform. One of the best known examples is provided by J.Z. Knight, who claims to be in touch with an old spirit-guide named Ramtha and whom thousands flock to hear imparting the ancient wisdom she claims is channelled through her. Other channellers have written books of such wisdom whilst in the trance-like state in which channellers habitually operate.

Why is channelling so important within the New Age movement? Clearly the air of mystery surrounding it attracts many of the curious. Those committed to it, however, believe it enables them to get to know themselves, what they are now, what they were in previous existences, and what they may become in some future state, for it is this information that those involved in channelling believe is being gleaned through this technique.[25] On the whole, the kind of information thus gathered appears to be very ordinary to warrant building upon it so high a view.

As with many psychic experiences, those who do not believe the claims of those receiving them try to explain them in a number of ways.

- Some argue that channellers, mediums and the like are often frauds, performing in a way that pleases people in order to earn money. Although this may be a explanation for some, it cannot account for them all.
- Drane suggests that in some cases channellers are not treated too seriously either by themselves or by their audiences. Both understand that what they are experiencing is the entertainment akin to a clever magician.[26]
- In contrast, some mainstream Christians believe that channelling should be treated very seriously indeed, because they believe the contacts made through this technique are satanical and are akin to the spiritualistic practices condemned outright in Deuteronomy 18.10-11: 'Let no one be found among you who makes his son or daughter pass through fire, no augur or soothsayer or diviner or sorcerer, no one who casts spells or traffics with ghosts and spirits, and no necromancer' (REB).
- Yet others would argue for a psychological explanation of channelling. In some cases, it is argued, the channellers are themselves suffering from mental disturbance and need treatment. More often than not, however, encouraged by their trance-like states, channellers may be latching on to something in their own psyches, digging deeply into their own unconscious.

No matter how the phenomenon is explained, channelling remains one of the best-known characteristics of New Age activity. It is usually justified on the basis that it has a long and honourable history in many major religious traditions. Corinne McLauglin, for example, sees examples of channelling 'from shamans among native and aboriginal peoples, to the Delphic oracles of ancient Greece, to Abraham and Moses in the Hebrew tradition, Joan of Arc in the Christian, and Joseph Smith in the Mormon tradition'.[27]

Witchcraft

Witchcraft, or Wiccan as its practitioners prefer to call it, claims to be the ancient religion that was unfairly and sometimes cruelly replaced by Christianity. It has seen something of a revival in New Age circles, particularly through the influence of Starhawk (Miriam Simos), the American feminist writer and white witch, whom William Bloom describes as 'the most influential New Age exponent of the religion and techniques of the Goddess and the Wiccan'.[28]

At the heart of Wiccan belief is the pantheistic view that the divine is all and all is the divine, and is usually focused on the Mother Goddess. In the case of Starhawk, this view of the divine is much more appealing than what she calls the patriarchy encouraged by celibate Christian clergy with their view that sexuality, and therefore woman, was 'dirty'. 'We are the Goddess', she tells her readers. 'We are each a part of the inter-penetrating, interconnecting reality that is All.'[29] 'Goddess religion', she continues, 'identifies sexuality as the expression of the creative force of the universe. It is not dirty, nor is it merely "normal"; it is sacred, the manifestation of the Goddess.' Because of this, 'All acts of love and pleasure are My rituals', says the Goddess. 'Sexuality is sacred because it is a sharing of energy, in passionate surrender to the power of the Goddess, immanent in our desire.' So Starhawk adds, 'In orgasm, we share in the force that moves the stars'.[30]

Wiccans claim they have thousands of followers in the United Kingdom. They may operate as solitary witches, engaging in a variety of occult practices in the privacy of their own homes. Coven witches, however, are more likely to come to the attention of the public at large. Whilst writing this book, for example, I was watching a local television news item about a controversy between Christians and Wiccans in Stevenage. The Wiccans had asked the local authority to allow them to practise their religion in a public place, on the grounds that they had the constitutional right to freedom of worship, whereas the Christians had asserted that this would be harmful to the community at large.

Coven witches meet in small groups of no more than thirteen people, usually in the open air after dark. They draw a sacred circle, and cleanse it from evil with the four elements of earth, air, fire and water. A priestess (or less frequently a priest) then uses a variety of techniques such as deep concentration, meditation, or trance, within the circle of witches, all looking inwards because they believe that the divine is within themselves, not an outside, independent deity. The aim is for the priestess to absorb the divinity of the Goddess into herself and to become more aligned with the spirits or devas behind the natural world. Witches expect some kind of inner transformation to occur as a result of this ritual and this may then lead to healings, clairvoyance, foretelling the future, or various forms of magic.

Witches sometimes get a bad press, not only because of the ideas of witches that have come down to us in literature, but also because people often confuse them with Satanists and accuse them of all kinds of evils, including human sacrifice and sexual orgies. No evidence of either is produced, though the initiation of a new witch does seem to require that those who form the circle should be naked and that the initiate should seal her membership with sexual intercourse. Wiccans say, however, that the sexual act is only symbolised, except where the two people involved are already sexual partners, and even then the rest of the circle disappear discreetly while it is happening.

Starhawk and other devotees of Wiccan claim antecedents for their practices in various religious traditions. Some Christians would identify Wiccan rituals seeking identification with the Goddess with the forbidden rituals directed towards the queen of heaven in the Old Testament. In Jeremiah 7.17-18 the prophet describes God's displeasure with such practices: *'Children are gathering wood, fathers lighting the fire, women kneading dough to make crescent cakes in honour of the queen of heaven; and drink offerings are poured out to other gods – all to grieve me'*. Most Christians would regard Deuteronomy 18.10-12 as a direct command against such religious activities, which they regard as idolatrous.

The Age of Aquarius

Astrology is thought to provide a historical point of reference for a more syncretistic spirituality and the rejection of organised religion, for an important plank in the New Age message is that we are moving from the Age of Pisces to the Age of Aquarius. In practical terms, this means we are moving from fixity to fluidity, from rigidity to tolerance. So, as we have seen, New Age challenges us to make a paradigm shift, a major change in our thinking, a distinctly new way of looking at things. This will lead to all kinds of other changes in the way we think and behave.

The need for individual and social transformation

Among the required changes are individual and social transformation. We must allow the new outlook to affect everything – medicine, business, marriage, leisure, religion, the lot. Full development of the individual's personality is an overriding concern of the movement. It is to do with what people feel more than with what they think. The message seems to be, 'Trust your feelings, your emotions, your experience, rather than your intellect'. Meditation and various other techniques will enable people to discover themselves and to blend with the 'Creative Intelligence'. The aim of all of this is to enable us to become integrated, fulfilled, and completely loving human beings.

This particular approach, which is an indication that New Age cannot be treated only as religion in the traditionally understood sense of that word, has attracted some of those responsible for the training of senior executives of multi-national companies. They claim that the use of New Age practitioners in training programmes improves the personal performance of senior staff. According to John Drane, 'Management consultants have spread the New Age message across the corporate world of business executives'.[31]

'God' in New Age thinking

Where God comes into all of this is problematical. No doubt those New Agers who move into New Age from a traditional Christian background take some traditional ideas of God with them. Others appear to have dispensed with God altogether. Those who cling to belief in God, which is probably still the majority, seem to have given up belief in a personal God, preferring impersonal terms like Life Force or Creative Intelligence, their views being built around the twin concepts of monism and pantheism both of which are much older than the New Age.

Monism, is the belief that reality is of one kind throughout, that there is an essential unity of all. Pantheism is the belief that the one reality of which monism speaks is God. In other words, God is that impersonal force or energy permeating everything. Clearly the two are interrelated and this throws some light on some of the practices characteristic of the New Age movement. Against the background of this kind of philosophy, it is to be expected that New Age followers regard the earth, not just as something to be treated with respect, but to be worshipped as the Mother Goddess, Gaia.

Crystals

Similarly, crystals become the vehicles for linking the energy which is at the heart of everything (and therefore as an agency for healing) to those people who take the trouble to find the kind of crystals to which they can relate. Because crystals are filled with celestial energy, they can bring physical and psychological healing and wholeness to those who use them. Some crystals are believed to have qualities which help with specific matters, such as amethyst which is said to increase self-confidence and to cure amnesia and headaches and quartz, which is believed to improve a person's creativity.

The 'feel good' factor

One of the major claims of the New Age movement is that it has broken away from the alleged shackles of the organised religion represented by Christianity and Judaism and has set people free to develop their own spirituality and behaviour patterns in a way that is meaningful for them individually. New Age leaders agree that we must leave aside the over cerebral approach of western culture which stemmed from the Enlightenment. For too long this has resulted in too many people adopting an unquestionning faith in the 'objective facts' propounded by a science which itself leaned far too heavily on Newtonian physics with its belief in unchanging laws. Now subjectivity is the order of the day, with its reliance on a right brain approach which takes account of feelings. When that approach is adopted, there seems to be no place for religious creeds or approved morality for all.

This accords well with the 'modern' approach, with its basic assumption that 'It's all right if it feels good for me'. What needs to be remembered, however, is that this particular stance concerning belief and behaviour is in itself an implied credal statement. As John Drane rightly points out, 'The conviction that subjective experience is more important than objective fact is itself a belief, which may or may not be true'.[32]

THE NEW AGE MOVEMENT AND CHRISTIANITY

New Agers, for all their tolerance and eclecticism, are firm in the belief that the crippling hold of Christianity – with its distinctive belief in God who is personal and whose incarnate Son is the world's Saviour – must be broken. Mainstream Christianity is a no-go area for many New Agers, for with Judaism, it represents the rigidity of that passing Age of Pisces which must give way to the new Age of Aquarius. A reasonable dialogue between the two is difficult to maintain, therefore, for one of the parties to the dialogue, New Age, has already written off the other, mainstream Christianity, as archaic, harmful and irrelevant. Nevertheless, such a dialogue must be pursued with New Age, as with the other religious movements in this book.

Mainstream Christians can respond in any one of three ways. The first is for Christians to adopt the same intolerant attitude to the New Age as some New Age followers adopt to Christianity, rejecting it out of hand. Some Christians do this, asserting that everything about New Age is of the devil. There is no place for dialogue, for that would be to compromise truth, so all that New Age believes and promotes must be rejected out of hand. A little reflection reveals that this approach cannot really be maintained. Many ideas found within New Age are shared with others, including Christians, and cannot be rejected. Others go to the other extreme. All roads lead to God, so let's welcome them aboard. As so often a middle way seems to be the best. We must recognise what is good and where we need to differ to do it with charity.

New Agers and Christians can agree that:

* There is an invisible and inner dimension to all life. Materialism must not be allowed the last word.
* There is a need for transformation – for fundamental change – both of the individual and of society. Jesus told Nicodemus, 'You must be born again'. He also preached the Gospel of the Kingdom of God, with its call to work for Kingdom values here and now and to look for the coming of the Kingdom in all its fullness in God's good time.
* Individual's should be encouraged freely to pursue their personal spiritual pilgrimage.
* There is much more to the individual person than most of us have either understood or seen. Growth towards potential is a challenge which Christians have to face.
* The whole ecological challenge and its call to responsible stewardship is something we should all support. It is built into Genesis 1. We are accountable to God for the way we use his world.

But there are some fundamental differences, as the following comparison makes clear.

WHERE NEW AGE AND CHRISTIANITY PART COMPANY

NEW AGE	CHRISTIANITY

Revelation

Truth (like everything else) is part of the Life Force which flows through everything. Truth is therefore something subjective. All that we need to know about 'God' and about ourselves is already within us. It is not laid down in credal statements. Each individual has to explore truth in total freedom and discover it through personal experience.

Truth comes from God, who has revealed the truth about himself and about ourselves in his incarnate Word, Jesus Christ, through his written word, the Bible. Doctrinal formularies and credal statements are accepted because the Church believes them to be in accordance with that divine revelation. Individually we make that truth our own through our experience of God in Christ.

God

The New Age concept of God is pantheistic. God is all and all is God. As the impersonal Life Force flowing through everything, God or the Mother Goddess, Gaia, is part of creation, and not distinct from or over and above it.

The Christian understanding of God is monotheistic and trinitarian. God is one, yet within the unity of the Godhead there are three divine persons, Father, Son and Holy Spirit. God is sovereign Lord of creation (transcendent), yet present in all that he has brought into being (immanent).

Christ

He is one of many spiritual teachers or guides to whom people can look for help in their spiritual pilgrimage, good people who through the ages have been special teachers and, in that sense, god-helpers.

Jesus Christ is the eternal Son of God, the unique Word of God who became incarnate when born of the Virgin Mary. He was sent by God to be not only our Teacher but also our Saviour.

NEW AGE	CHRISTIANITY

Salvation

All that is needed to transform the individual into a complete and fulfilled person lies within that person. Individually, we discover that we are part of the All, the unity which holds everything together, that we are 'God'. We need no outside Saviour, though any of a variety of techniques may help us to make that great self-discovery. When ignorance is dispelled, human potential is fulfilled, and we become complete persons.

Our fundamental problem is that our human nature is flawed. Although made by God for fellowship with and service for him, our shortcomings (sin) separate us from him and prevent us from being the kind of people we are meant to be. Christ is the God-given Saviour. Through turning from sin (repenting) and putting our faith in him (trusting) we are brought back into a right relationship with God and begin to become the kind of people God has always wanted us to be.

The Future

The journey of self-discovery will not be accomplished in a single life-span, but through a series of reincarnations, for this life is one in a series of many. Progress through our reincarnated lives depends upon our own efforts. When we finally escape from this cycle of lives, we shall be united with the Life Force.

Eternal life is God's gift of grace, not a reward for work done. We respond to God's offer of life in Christ in this life and begin the spiritual journey towards our full potential in the here and now. We trust God to bring us to our full potential in eternity.

NEW AGE   CHRISTIANITY

Communication

Channelling, witchcraft, astrology, meditation, and other New Age techniques and practices provide the guidance and help we need for our spiritual pilgrimage.

Through Christ Christians believe they have been brought into a loving relationship with God. Their fellowship with him and with their fellow Christians grows through worship, communion, prayer, meditation, and in other ways.

Boundaries

There are none, either in belief or practice. Individuals must find their own way. They are free to choose from any past or present religious tradition or non-religious system. They select what suits them from this wide range of options, some of which appear to be inconsistent and contradictory.

God has shown us the boundaries of faith and practice in Christ and through the Bible. Belief and behaviour must be based on that revelation. If that is done, channelling, witchcraft and astrology will be rejected.

These brief summaries of areas of agreement and disagreement between New Age and mainstream Christianity indicate the need for Christians to become more informed about what is rapidly becoming perhaps the most attractive and therefore the most significant of the contemporary alternatives to traditional Christianity.[33]

REFERENCES

1. William Bloom, *The New Age – An Anthology of Essential Writings*, pub. Channel Four.
2. Eileen Barker, *New Religious Movements*, pub. HMSO, page 189.
3. John Drane, *What is the New Age saying to the Church?*, pub. Marshall Pickering, 1991, page 18.
4. W. Bloom op. cit. page xvi.

5. Michael Perry, *Gods Within*, pub. SPCK 1992, page 5.
6. M. Perry, op. cit. page 19.
7. op. cit. page 4.
8. Bloom, op cit. page 2.
9. Bloom., op. cit. page 22.
10. Bloom, op. cit. pages 21f.
11. Bloom, op. cit. page 23.
12. Marilyn Ferguson, *The Aquarian Conspiracy*, pub. Paladin 1982, page 27.
13. Ferguson, op. cit. page 156.
14. Ferguson, op. cit. page 83.
15. Ferguson, op. cit. page 26.
16. Bloom, op. cit. page 2.
17. Perry, op. cit. page 33.
18. *Sweet Inspiration*, pages 102f.
19. Bloom, op. cit. page xvii.
20. ibid.
21. ibid.
22. *Sweet Inspiration*, page 106.
23. ibid.
24. ibid.
25. Drane, op. cit. page 112.
26. Drane, op. cit. page 115.
27. Bloom, op. cit. page 51.
28. Bloom, op. cit. page 228.
29. Bloom, op. cit. page 34.
30. Bloom, op. cit. page 35.
31. Drane, op. cit. page 43.
32. Drane, op. cit. page 70.
33. Drane, op. cit. page 25.

A CHRISTIAN
RESPONSE

We have examined seven religious alternatives to mainstream Christianity, seen how they originated, noted their distinctive beliefs and practices, and discovered where those beliefs and practices are similar to, and distinct from, mainstream Christianity. With that background, we are now able to consider the appropriate Christian response to be made to these and similar fringe movements. At least four responses are possible, and with varying degrees of emphasis all of them can be seen in church history and the life of the contemporary Church. Mainstream Christians can deliberately ignore fringe groups, totally reject them, uncritically accept them, or can enter into intelligent dialogue with them.

At first sight the easiest option seems to be that of completely ignoring fringe groups. Many of these alternatives to the mainstream, it can be argued, spring up overnight under the leadership of a charismatic-type figure, blossom for a short time, and then fade away into oblivion when the leader dies. If we wait long enough, the problem will go away. Too often the Church has tried to deal with its problems in this rather arrogant way, and it never works.

It will not work with fringe groups for at least three reasons. First, it does not accord with the facts to say that all such groups have a limited life-span. Whilst some of the more bizarre cults do disappear with the death of their leader, other fringe groups (such as the Mormons, Jehovah's Witnesses, Christadelphians, and Christian Science, examined in earlier chapters) persist to become established sects. Secondly, it is a fact that contemporary fringe groups recruit many of their members from the ranks of disillusioned members of mainstream churches. They often turn to these alternative groups because in their view the Church is not offering what they are looking for, whether it is an appropriate spirituality, clear teaching, a warm and welcoming community life, or a relevant approach to the problems of the world and its people. Thirdly, many active church members have relatives involved in such alternative groups, and even those not in that position are likely to receive visits from fringe group missionaries from time to time. It will not do, therefore, for the Church to adopt an ostrich-like stance, for it looks as if fringe groups are here to stay, they are winning over church members, and church members are concerned.

The second option is for Christians to totally reject fringe movements and their members and all that they stand for. After all, that in the main is the way fringe groups treat mainstream Christianity, regarding it as apostate, erroneous, satanical, irrelevant, and in some instances all four! Some sincere but, I believe, misguided Christians have similar views about fringe groups, asserting that everything about them is wrong, their leaders are evil, and the devil is working through both leaders and led. That being the case, the less we have to do with them the better. As I shall seek to demonstrate, this attitude of rejecting them all lock, stock and barrel is impossible to sustain.

Realising that complete rejection would mean throwing out the baby with the bathwater, some mainstream Christians go to the other extreme. No human organisation has all the truth, they say. Even those within the mainstream do not agree about everything. Exclusivism must give way to inclusivism. Adherents of the major world religions, those on the fringes of these religions, and many others not linked with any particular religious group, are all feeling after the same divine reality. Whether they describe that reality in personal terms, like God in Christianity and Judaism, or in impersonal terms, like 'Ultimate Reality' or 'World Soul' as in eastern religions and some western offshoots, is relatively unimportant. In short, all roads lead to God, so let's welcome them all , no matter what they call themselves, as fellow seekers after truth. By adopting this approach we shall affirm each other's insights and traditions, and learn from them all.

This approach is as difficult to sustain as that of complete rejection. Whereas the former sees nothing good in anything outside mainstream Christianity, the latter fails to take seriously those very different and often contradictory beliefs which these religious movements themselves are quick to point out. Learn from each other, we must, but we must also take each tradition seriously, whether its followers number hundreds of millions (as with Christianity and other world religions) or a few hundred (as with the Family). Nothing is to be gained by blurring the distinctions.

So we are left with the fourth option, that of entering into intelligent dialogue with fringe groups. This would seem to be the most constructive approach. Christians should acknowledge and affirm the areas of agreement, be clear about the areas of disagreement, and be willing to discuss these in an intelligent manner.

AREAS OF AGREEMENT

We all believe there is a spiritual dimension to life. The seven alternatives and mainstream Christians agree that human beings need to recognise and develop this spiritual dimension if they are to become the people they are capable of becoming.

We all believe that men and women need to be changed. The preferred terminology may vary, including 'salvation', 'new birth', 'enlightenment', 'fulfilment', 'wholeness', and so on. Behind it all, however, is the common conviction that there is more to life than the physical, and that men and women need to be changed. Although we all offer different solutions to the problem, there is agreement about the need for a transformation to take place.

We all have the Bible. Jehovah's Witnesses, Christadelphians, Mormons, Christian Science, the Children of God, and the Unification Church, share with mainstream Christians the belief that in the Bible we have the Word of God, even though they reject the Christian interpretation of the Bible upon which the historic Christian creeds are based. New Age, though not accepting the Bible as authoritative in the way that Christians and these other six movements regard it, nevertheless recognise that the Bible contains ancient wisdom which should not be ignored.

Here are three areas of belief in which there is at least some common ground between mainstream Christians and the seven fringe groups. As we look at each group specifically, we shall find that there are others on which Christianity and that particular group stand on common ground. These areas of agreement should be acknowledged and affirmed. They form a useful starting point for any attempts at dialogue.

MAJOR DIFFERENCES

Our earlier examination of each fringe movement in turn has revealed in some detail a number of significant differences between each group and mainstream Christianity, regarding both the group's doctrines and its practices. This final chapter simply provides an opportunity to gather together the common differences from Christianity which all or most of the groups share .

The Trinity

With the exception of the Family (the Children of God), they each explicitly or implicitly deny the doctrine of the Trinity. Because some of them continue to use trinitarian-type terminology, however, it is important to be clear what Christians mean by Trinity. Briefly, Christians believe that God is one, yet that within the unity of the Godhead there are three divine Persons, the Father, the Son, and the Holy Spirit. Each is God, yet there are not three Gods but one God. The three divine Persons are co-equal and co-eternal.

Now this is clearly not what the fringe groups believe. Though Mormons, Jehovah's Witnesses, Christian Science, Christadelphians, and the Unification Church all speak of Father, Son, and Holy Spirit, their writings make it quite clear that the meanings attached to such terminology are different from those of Christians, as can be confirmed by reference to earlier chapters of this book. Jehovah's Witnesses, in fact, state categorically that they believe the Christian doctrine of the Trinity is derived from ancient mythology and is of the devil. Though New Age also seems to be happy to include some Christians within its ranks, it has settled for a pantheistic view of an impersonal Life Force or World Soul, which again is very far removed from the Christian doctrine of the Trinity.

The Person and Work of Christ

Nobody studying the Christian faith can be left with any doubt concerning the central place occupied by Jesus Christ and the exclusiveness of the claims made about him. God's plan for human and cosmic redemption is shown to be focused in his person, as the incarnate Son of God, and brought about through his work of atonement as the crucified and resurrected Saviour. The uniqueness of Christ's person and work is summed up particularly in the New Testament words, 'For in him God in all his fullness chose to dwell and through him to reconcile all things to himself, making peace through the shedding of his blood on the cross – all things, whether on earth or in heaven'. Or again, 'It is in Christ that the Godhead in all its fullness dwells embodied, it is in him you have been brought to fulfilment' (Colossians 1.19-20; 2.9-10 REB).

When comparing this mainstream Christian view with the position given to Christ in the seven alternatives to the mainstream in this book, the Family are again seen to be the odd one out. Their view of Christ seems fairly orthodox from a Christian point of view, and in their early Children of God days they sprang out of the American Jesus Movement and were thought to be straightforward evangelical Christians. In reality, however, the place of Jesus Christ has been overshadowed (some would say usurped) by their founder, David Berg. He, rather than Christ, became the focus of members' commitment.

As we have seen in earlier chapters, five of the others, Mormons, Jehovah's Witnesses, Christadelphians, Christian Science, and the

Unification Church, reject the Christian view, all denying that Christ is God incarnate and the Unification Church denying that he is Saviour. For New Age, Christ is not a central figure at all, but is relegated to the position of one great teacher among many others, all of whom have contributed to the spiritual development of the human race.

Salvation

Here again there are some marked differences between Christians and the seven alternatives. Christians believe that humanity's basic problem is that it is flawed by sin and that sin separates people from God. In short, therefore, Christians believe that if human beings are to be the kind of people God always intended them to be, they need to be brought back into a right relationship with God . The New Testament makes clear how this reconciliation with all its positive spin-offs is to be brought about: 'It is by grace you are saved through faith; it is not your own doing. It is God's gift, not a reward for work done. There is nothing for anyone to boast of; we are God's handiwork, created in Christ Jesus for the life of good deeds which God designed for us' (Ephesians 2.8-10 REB).

In contrast to this doctrine of salvation by grace through faith, all seven fringe groups offer their respective ways of salvation, wholeness, enlightenment, or fulfilment as a reward for their members' participation in their respective practices or techniques. Nothing could be further removed from the Christian view that out of love Christ sent his Son to be the world's Saviour.

The position of Christianity

There is one more doctrinal obstacle to be overcome if Christians are to be able to enter into an intelligent dialogue with members belonging to fringe movements on the Christian perimeter. It stems from the general attitude of fringe groups to Christianity, or Christendom as some of them prefer to call it.

New Age followers treat mainstream Christianity as if it has very little to offer in the search for truth, as if it were completely irrelevant to the needs of twentieth century men and women. In contrast, they see themselves as very much in tune with the final decade of the twentieth century, and in particular try to blend their more esoteric beliefs with a mixture of new science. The other six fringe groups are much more simplistically clear about their relations with mainstream Christianity. Each of them seems to believe that it alone is the only truly Christian movement and with varying degrees of vehemence state that the divided mainstream Christian churches are in error, or are deliberately apostate, or are of the devil. This is not a helpful stance to be confronted with by any Christians willing to discuss differences in a charitable and intelligent manner.

Quite apart from major doctrinal differences, any Christian wishing to enter into meaningful dialogue with sects, cults, and new religious movements will also need to be aware of problems about some of the methods fringe groups use and practices they adopt.

Among these, perhaps the biggest cause of concern are the 'hard sell' methods some of them use to win converts. These may take the form of intensive psychological programming techniques, or the use of overzealous and aggressive proselytising methods. These have without doubt left some deep emotional and psychological scars on some of those subjected to them, as interviews with former members soon reveal. Some who break away vow never to have dealings with any kind of religion again. Parents of cult members describe what they call the 'personality change' they have witnessed as their sons or daughters become more deeply involved in some of these groups, or the zombie-like state into which they have lapsed. What should be healthy and wholesome commitment has degenerated into such an obsessional state that some observers have described it as a hypnotic or trance-like state, and have tried to explain its cause as intensive and unrelenting indoctrination over periods of several hours at a time. Linked with this is the practice used by some of these groups in trying to separate members from their natural families, their former friends, and in some instances to persuade them to give up their studies or employment.

Then there is what is sometimes called 'the rip-off factor'. With the Children of God this has taken the form of persuading members to 'spoil the Egyptians', that is to get their relatives to part with as much money as possible so that it can be ploughed into the cult. At a different level, some New Age followers have been as concerned as many outside that movement at the way some unscrupulous people have cashed in on the craze for crystals and other New Age artefacts, charging exorbitant prices because of the alleged benefits to health and wholeness that come from such objects.

A number of other practices found within the New Age movement are by nature the kind that mainstream Christians will find equally disturbing. As noted in chapter 7, they include the use of tarot cards and ouija boards, and the practice of witchcraft, channelling and astrology.

No realistic dialogue can occur between the mainstream Christian Church and any of these fringe groups without an honest attempt to face and discuss such difficulties.

THE CHALLENGE

The major differences in doctrine and practice summarised above indicate that the fourth option, that of seeking to enter into charitable and intelligent dialogue with Mormons, Jehovah's Witnesses, Christadelphians, Christian Scientists, The Family, The Unification Church, and New Age, is a difficult aim to achieve. Viewed alongside the other options of deliberately ignoring, totally rejecting, and uncritically accepting them, however, it is a far more honest and positively Christian response. What kind of a challenge does this present to the churches and to individual church members?

The Churches

At present almost all the research into what most of them now prefer to call new religious movements is being doing by sociologists. Understandably they are not always as concerned as the mainstream churches about the theology of such groups. Church responses to fringe groups usually come from two sources, those who have become members of Christian churches after leaving one of these alternative groups, and other freelance Christian writers. The former are helpful in that they provide useful insights from those who have been involved, but they are inevitably subjective and sometimes rather extreme in their judgements. The latter are not always as well researched as they might be, and are sometimes light on theology. The mainstream Christian churches, probably at national level and working ecumenically, should as a matter of policy encourage and resource one or two people with the necessary theological background to research and write about the sects, cults and other movements presenting alternatives to the mainstream. With this kind of back-up, local churches would be much more equipped to prepare members for the challenge they face when meeting those belonging to groups on the Christian fringe.

Local churches should take very positive steps to ensure that members are better educated about the doctrines of the Christian faith, as well as about Christian practice. Members of fringe groups normally put Christians to shame with their grasp of their own basic teachings, practices and techniques, and their ability to share what they believe with others. Sometimes they can even hold their own in discussion because they have an informed view of mainstream Christianity. In contrast, most Christians struggle when they are asked to defend what they believe. They need to become more informed, and it is the local churches responsibility to ensure that they are so informed.

Local church members

Although the churches have their responsibility, it is the individual Christian and the members of his or her family who are more likely to come into face-to-face contact with members of fringe groups. These are the people who will receive doorstep visits from Jehovah's Witnesses or Mormons; who may come into contact with Christian Scientists through claims of healing; or who could be attracted to attend Christadelphian Bible exhibitions held in a local public hall. It is these Christians who are likely to be affected by the large amount of explicit or (more likely) implicit media coverage given to New Age ideas; or who may find a member of their family or the family of a friend involved with the Unification Church or The Family. And it is these same individual church members who will need to be ready with a Christian response.

Are there guidelines which might help them in such situations? There are, but at the risk of sounding patronising or alarmist I wish to suggest that people without a strong grasp of their own Christian faith would be well advised to tread very carefully when dealing with members of fringe groups. Patiently and politely refuse all overtures designed to involve you in fringe groups. Do not invite their members into your home, or become involved in any of their study groups or courses, and treat their literature with caution. Bring the encounter to an end as soon as possible; and be determined to learn more about the faith you yourself profess.

Guidelines for committed Christians

1. The first requirement is that you should know what you believe and be ready to speak about your faith in a clear way. This does not mean that you need to become an amateur theologian, or that necessarily God has given you the gift of evangelism. But it does mean that you may need to spend a little more time than most Christians are prepared to give learning more of what it means to be a Christian, and exploring Christian belief and practice. You need to do this, whether or not you are ever likely to meet members of fringe reli- gions. It is particularly important, however, if you do meet them for

without it you will speedily be at a disadvantage. Most members of sects, cults or new religious movements are well versed in their group's teaching and will want to challenge you about your faith.

2. As a committed Christian you should remember that in dealing with members of fringe groups you are dealing with those who, like you and all other human beings, are made in the image of God. As a fellow human being, you should wish to treat them courteously, politely, patiently, and without aggression. As a Christian, you should treat them with the same love, concern and respect that your Christian faith teaches you to treat all men and women, whatever their colour, class, or creed. Unless you are willing to do this, it would be better to avoid them altogether, for any other attitude is almost certainly going to be counter productive.

3. Do not question their sincerity. In this connection, it is worth remembering that many members of sects, cults and new religious movements have turned to these groups after failing to find what they were searching for in mainstream Christian churches. Discussions with a number of them over many years have led me to believe that they are at least as sincere about their faith as I am about mine.

4. You should be ready to listen carefully to your fringe contacts, question them sensitively, try to discover how and why they joined their group, what they think it offers them, and what makes them tick. You cannot be expected to carry in your head the beliefs and practices of all five hundred of the sects, cults and new religious movements which are said to be active in Britain today! But if you know your own faith, you will soon pick up the major differences in the faith of your fringe contacts – and if you meet them more than once you should have an opportunity to discover more about them in the interval!

5. Though you should know what you believe and want to share it with sensitivity, do your utmost to avoid bitter arguments, especially about doctrine. Christian witness is not about winning arguments. If your contacts belong to groups that seem to set great store by the Bible, do not allow yourself to be drawn into the silly game of 'Bible ping-pong', where texts are torn out of context, twisted to mean almost anything other than what they clearly mean in their context, and used as weapons between you. You should not indulge in slanging matches about the love of God!

6. Avoid the temptation to indulge in the kind of character assassination which has all too often been a characteristic of those who oppose

fringe groups. You may have your own views about some cult leaders, but it will serve no useful purpose in being forthright in your condemnation of them to their followers. If they have the kind of unquestioning devotion to their leaders that, for example, members of The Family show to David Berg, Christian Scientists give to Mary Baker Eddy, or members of the Unification Church have for Sun Myung Moon, vitriolic attacks may merely help to convince them that mainstream Christianity is evil, as they have been taught. In any case, people who live in glass houses ... ! Even mainstream Christian leaders are not always without blemish.

7. When your contacts have 'preached' their message to you, as most of them will want to do, ask questions in an attempt to get them to restate it in ordinary, jargon free language. Do anything that encourages them to think hard about their views, rather than simply accepting them uncritically which is what most fringe groups expect of their members,

8. Aim to show your contacts that there is much more to life than the narrowly religious shell in which some of them will be trapped. Talk to them about themselves, their family, and about the world from which many of them have retreated.

9. Talk to them about what it means to you to be a Christian. Try to show them that your faith is not the deadly formal or irrelevant thing that some fringe groups claim Christianity to be, but a living and fulfilling experience of God through Christ. Tell them (if it is true) that your local church is a warm, loving, and accepting Christian community, which helps you to be yourself and nourishes your faith.

10. Be patient! As with all other forms of Christian outreach, time is needed to build up the relationships in which positive dialogue is able to occur. This presupposes that fringe contacts are willing to enter into dialogue, rather than simply wanting to convert you, but unfortunately that is by no means always the case. Experience shows that some groups warn off members when they begin to become involved in honest dialogue built on growing relationships.

Guidelines for those with relatives involved in fringe groups

There are particular problems for those whose close relatives become members of fringe groups and either cut themselves off from their family or become more remote and distant in their family relationships. It is not at all unusual to hear of young men or women in their early twenties who join one of the newer fringe religious groups, give up promising careers or university places, leave home, and virtually disown their parents. There are other instances of married people who join one of the more established fringe groups and, although they continue to live at home, have changed their beliefs and lifestyles so radically that they now have little or nothing in common with their partners. In such circumstances, what were once happy marriages are in danger of coming to an end.

Parents or partners of fringe group members can then begin to display some of the classical symptoms of bereavement. They feel forsaken, betrayed, and usually very angry. They often articulate such feelings in words like, 'How can he/she behave like this after all I have done for her/him?' They are then tempted to over-react, sometimes even threatening to disown the son or daughter or to end the marriage. Understandable though such feelings and reactions may be, they are unhelpful to both the fringe group member and the parent or partner.

How should parents and husbands or wives respond in such circumstances? A better way is needed. Much of what has been written earlier in this chapter will be relevant to such situations, but a few other suggestions may be appropriate.

1. Become better informed

Before doing anything else, take the trouble to learn more about the fringe group which you son, daughter or marriage partner has joined. Many books are available, and organizations like FAIR – Family, Action, Information and Resource (BCM Box 3535, PO Box 12, London WC1N 3XX) and INFORM (10 Portugal Street, London WC2A 2HD) are always ready to help. And there are always your local church leaders. When you have done your homework, you will be ready to discuss the group's origins, beliefs, moral stance, and methods of outreach with your involved relative in as fair minded a way as possible. Avoid bitter arguments, which are usually counter-product. A calmer discussion, especially if well thought-out questions are asked, may encourage your relative to think about important issues about his or her involvement in the group never previously considered. It has been known for worried relatives to discover in this process that the group which their child or partner has joined is not after all an unorthodox fringe group but a branch of mainstream Christianity. You may discover that you are not as far apart as you thought. Even when this is not the case, nothing has been lost and much gained by taking the trouble to ensure that you are well-informed about the group concerned.

2. Think before you speak or act

This is easier said than done. When dealing with relatives involved in fringe groups matters often come to a head quite unexpectedly. For example, a son or daughter 'disappears' and is then found living communally with fellow-members of the group. This is often the case when the involvement is with one of the newer groups. Or a marriage partner wants to dip into the family savings to pursue an expensive training course. Yet again, a partner may become so deeply immersed in a group that he or she ceases to give time to spouse or children. If this attitude persists, proceedings for divorce and the custody of the children may soon follow.

These and similar occurrences are standard issues handled regularly by those counselling worried relatives. Unfortunately, it often happens that much of the damage has been done to the relationship before a counsellor is consulted. Angry words have been used, pointless threats have been made, and the relationship has deteriorated almost beyond remedy. So try to avoid reaching this impasse. Think carefully before you speak or act.

3. Keep the lines of communication open

This again is not as easy as it sounds. Some of those involved in fringe groups can become obsessively secretive, an attitude sometimes encouraged by their leaders. For example, young people who have left home to join fringe groups may refuse to tell their parents where they are staying or what they are doing. Or married people may become so involved with the teaching and activities of their fringe group that it seems to be all that they are interested in. They withdraw from normal social activities and family life, and become very 'distant'. One reason for such attitudes is that for some fringe group members the only reality seems to be that which they experience within the fringe group. This makes it all the more important for their parents and partners to keep in touch with them and to keep them in contact with that other world from which they have withdrawn – the world of family life, work, leisure and other interests. The lesson is clear. Keep the normal lines of communication open.

How can this be done? If they are still living at home, by making special efforts to engage in conversation. Be ready to listen as well as to talk. Show that you are interested to hear why they have linked up with a fringe group and what belonging to it means to them. At the same time, share your concerns with them sincerely and without acrimony. If they are no longer living at home, write to them regularly, with all the family news and tell them about their friends. Although they may have given the impression that they are no longer interested, do not take this at its face value. Where possible, telephone and visit them. And try to make it clear that you love them and are concerned for them.

4. Remember that people do leave fringe groups

Those who join are not necessarily committed for life. Such groups, especially those which attract the 18 to 25 age range, have a high turn-over in membership. Though it may not be much of a consolation to you now, it is worth remembering that it is not unusual for members to stay for only two or three years before leaving of their own accord. Provided you have done your best to keep the lines of communication open and have continued to show them your love and concern, they will know where to turn when, often completely disillusioned, they leave the group. They will then need your support as they try to pick up the pieces and rebuild their lives.

5. Resist the use of force

There is always the temptation to resort to strong arm tactics in an attempt to 'rescue' a relative. Some people have set themselves up as de-programmers and their methods often involve forcibly removing a sect member, keeping him or her as a virtual prisoner and subjecting that person to a kind of intensive indoctrination in reverse for as long as it takes to persuade him or her to disown the leadership, teachings and practices of the offending sect or cult. Although it is understandable that worried relatives may wish to do almost anything to deliver their loved ones from what they believe are the evils inherent in membership of some fringe groups, it is important to remember that all of us have a God-given right to choose. Some forms of de-programming are no better than the intensive indoctrination of which fringe groups are often accused.

6. Be honest with yourself

Distressed relatives will not welcome my raising of this issue, but it needs to be faced. If you are a parent, it is worth asking yourself what other areas of your son's or daughter's life you would wish to decide for them – for example, their choice of job or career, their friends, their potential wives or husbands. If in these areas also you feel that father or mother knows best, this should sound alarm bells also in religious matters. Marriage partners will need to ask themselves related, but different, questions.

7. Respect individual freedom

However sure of our ground we may think we are, no matter how convinced we may be that our actions are in the best long term interest of others, we have no right to try to compel them to do what we want rather than what they want. In the last resort, the individual (whether son, daughter, partner, or anyone else) must be free to decide about his or her own religious affiliation or lack of it. This is often a hard lesson for parents and partners to learn, especially if they themselves are committed Christians with strong views about belief and behaviour. At the heart of the Christian message, however, is the belief that God does not compel any of us to trust and obey him. He gives all of us a choice. Unless we think we know better than God, we can do no less with our children, partners, or anyone else.

8. Pray

Prayer is placed last, not because it is the last resort but because it must not be used as an excuse for not following any of the other suggestions. Nevertheless, committed Christians will believe that this is their strongest weapon and will continue to use it when other tactics appear to be having no effect.

Try to imagine your relative's situation – his or her thoughts and feelings, beliefs and doubts, anxieties and fears, ambitions and ideals. You may not know where he or she is, but God knows. Surround your loved one with regular and consistent prayer. Even when there appears to be no answer, go on praying. Even more than you, God wants what is best for your son, daughter or marriage partner. Trust in him.

BIBLIOGRAPHY

L. Arrington and D. Bitton, *The Mormon Experience*, George Allen and Unwin, 1979.

J.J. Andrew, *The Real Christ*, The Dawn Book Supply, 1948.

Eileen Barker, *New Religious Movements*, HMSO Books, 1989.

David Berg, *Mo-Letters* (circulated by The Children of God/The Family).

W. Berrett, *The Restored Church*, Deseret Book Company, 1965.

William Bloom, *The New Age - An Anthology of Essential Writings*, A Channel Four book.

Fawn Brodie, *No Man Knows My History*, Knopf 1971.

Colin Brown, *Philosophy and the Christian Faith*, Tyndale Press, 1971.

M.C. Burrell, *Authority in Two Religious Sects*, Lancaster University Ph.D.

Church of England Doctrine Commission's Report, *Christian Believing*.

Christian Science: a Sourcebook of Contemporary Materials, the Christian Science Publishing Society, 1990.

M. Cole and others, *What is the New Age?*, Hodder and Stoughton, 1984.

John Drane, *What is the New Age saying to the Church?*, Marshall Pickering, 1991.

Mary Baker Eddy, *Church Manual of the First Church of Christ Scientist*, The Trustees under the will of Mary Baker Eddy.

Mary Baker Eddy, *Science and Health with Key to the Scriptures*, the First Church of Christ Scientist, Boston, USA.

C. Evans, *Cults of Unreason*, Harrap London, 1973.

Marilyn Ferguson, *The Aquarian Conspiracy*, Paladin, 1982.

A. Hoekema, *The Four Major Cults*, Paternoster Press, 1963.

Dewitt John, *The Christian Science Way of Life*, the Christian Science Publishing Society, Boston, 1962.

Young Oon Kim, *The Divine Principle and its Application*, The Holy Spirit Association for the Unification of World Christianity.

T.L. Leishmann, *Why I am a Christian Scientist*, Thomas Nelson and Sons, USA, 1958.

Warren Lewis in *A Time for Consideration*, ed. Bryant and Richardson, The Edwin Mellen Press, New York 1978.

W.R. Martin, *The Maze of Mormonism*, Zondervan 1962.

David O. McKay, *Gospel Ideals*, Church of Jesus Christ of Latter-day Saints, Salt Lake City.

Sun Myung Moon, *Divine Principle*, Holy Spirit Association for the Unification of World Christianity, 1973.

Sun Myung Moon, *The New Future of Christianity*, Holy Spirit Association for the Unification of World Christianity, 1974.

Mormon Media Pack 1.

Mormon Media Pack 5.

R. Mullen, *The Mormons*, W.H. Allen 1967.

E.J. Newman, *Jesus the Son of God* (A Christadelphian pamplet).

E.J. Newman, *The Doctrine of the Trinity* (A Christadelphian pamplet).

E.J. Newman, *The God Whom We Worship* (A Christadelphian pamplet).

Thomas O'Dea, *The Mormons*, University of Chicago Press, 1957.

Michael Perry, *Gods Within*, SPCK, 1992 .

Le Grand Richards, *A Marvelous Work and a Wonder*, Deseret Book Company 1956.

Robert Roberts, *The Blood of Christ*, The Christadelphian, Birmingham.

Robert Roberts, *Christendon Astray*, The Dawn Book Supply, 1958.

J.F. Rutherford, *The Harp of God* , Watch Tower Bible and Tract Society, 1928.

William Shaw, *Spying in Guru Land*, Fourth Estate, 1994.

Joseph Smith, *Doctrine and Covenants and Pearl of Great Price*, The Church of Jesus Christ of Latter-day Saints, Utah, 1952.

Joseph Smith, *The Book of Mormon*, The Church of Jesus Christ of Latter-day Saints, Utah, 1950.

Peter Spink, *A Christian in the New Age*, Darton, Longman and Todd, 1991.

J.E. Talmage, *Articles of Faith*, Mormon Church 1908.

John Thomas, *Elpis Israel*, The Christadelphian, Birmingham, 1958.

J.W.C. Wand, *The Four Great Heresies*, Mowbray, London, 1957.

Max Weber, *The Theory of Social and Economic Organisation*, Collier Macmillan, 1964.

Bryan Wilson, *Religious Sects*, World University Library, 1970.

Bryan Wilson, *Sects and Society*, Heinemann, 1961.

The following books are all published anonymously by the Watch Tower Bible & Tract Society, Brooklyn, USA. The more recent books are very largely a rewriting of the earlier ones. *Let God Be True* still provides a comprehensive introduction to Jehovah's Witness teaching.

Let God be True, 1962.

Make Sure of All Things, 1953.

Qualified to be Ministers, 1955.

Jehovah's Witnesses in the Divine Purpose, 1959.
Let Your Name Be Sanctified, 1961.
1992 Yearbook of Jehovah's Witnesses.
1995 Yearbook of Jehovah's Witnesses.
Your Word is a Lamp to My Foot.
Things in Which it is Impossible for God to Lie.
The Nations Shall Know that I am Jehovah, 1971.
You Can Live Forever in Paradise on Earth, 1989.